OTHER BOOKS BY GARY GRAF

And God Said, "Play Ball!"

LIGUORI, 2005

"'*Play Ball!*' does a splendid job of making us think about how life imitates sport....Delightfully tongue-in-cheek...carefully crafted to provide a context in which we can consider whether we are on God's team."

JOHN RAWLINGS, *THE SPORTING NEWS*

"With wit, some great baseball stories and a good head for analysis, Graf helps readers ponder the mysteries of life and baseball....It's all in good fun, but with a passion to help people find inspiration both on the playing field and in the Bible."

ST. LOUIS POST-DISPATCH

"...Perfect gift for the fan who has everything."

THE BIBLE TODAY

"...Easy reading, intelligent, and illuminating."

CATHOLIC NEW YORK

"Graf has cleverly blended major league baseball and the Bible into a very entertaining and highly informative book, which will lead even the casual reader to a greater appreciation of the world of both sport and Spirit....People seeking solace and strength through God's written word can find new inspiration and meaning in an unusual setting and a whole different cast of players."

NORMAN J. MUCKERMAN, C.SS.R., FORMER PRESIDENT, CATHOLIC PRESS ASSOCIATION

"...An ark load of witty and insightful parallels between the Bible and the national pastime."

"*'Play Ball!'* pulls off a near-miracle—an entirely fresh perspective on baseball, accomplished with wit and insight. The parallels between baseball and the Bible are fascinating."

"*'And God Said Play Ball!'* is a good parable about life. Gary Graf's love for baseball and love for his faith have helped him forge a vision of life that calls us to be thrilled by the challenges and opportunities that come our way in the nine innings of our lives."

"A good work of Scripture study and a fun recollection of the great moments and characters of the game...a delightful read."

"...Graf uses the game just as a composer might use his music, or a painter might use his oils, in bringing his audience closer to God."

"Author Gary Graf binds together religion and baseball as tightly as a baseball is wrapped with string and leather. Graf uses cogent baseball stories and stats to show how the great theological virtues of faith, hope, and love can be found in a dugout, on a ball field or in the stands."

"The deeper meaning Graf is getting at will keep you reading....The conversational tone the author takes in laying out his thoughts and observations will help anyone from a high school student in a religion class to a seasoned theologian...."

AND GOD SAID, "IT'S GOOD!"

I press on toward the goal for the prize...

PHILIPPIANS 3:14

"A deft feel for the inherent joy and mirth in sports and religion makes Gary Graf's books so endearing. Graf applies lessons in Christianity with neither brimstone nor fire but rather with the gentle rub of glove oil into a mitt as in *And God Said, "Play Ball!"* or a gentle dab of eye black in *And God Said, "It's Good!"*...Like any good coach, Graf gives his players, we fellow Christians and sports fans, a tap on the helmet, an arm around the shoulder, and a pat on the shoulder pads. He invites us to study up on the playbook that will lead us to lifelong victory...God's word."
—*The Sporting News*

Gary Graf's bestseller, *And God Said, "Play Ball!"*, opened the door to a wonderful array of connections between baseball and the Bible. He continues this appealing and revealing approach with *And God Said, "It's Good!"*— *Amusing and Thought-Provoking Parallels Between the Bible and Football.* Sunday morning Scripture students and Monday morning quarterbacks will delight in Graf's insights, humor, and knowledge. Enjoy!

AND GOD SAID, "IT'S GOOD!"

Amusing and Thought-Provoking Parallels Between the Bible and Football

Gary Graf

Liguori

Imprimi Potest:
Thomas D. Picton, CSsR
Provincial, Denver Province
The Redemptorists

Published Liguori Publications
Liguori, Missouri 63057
liguori.org

Library of Congress Cataloging-in-Publication Data

Graf, Gary.
    And God said, "It's good!" : amusing and thought-provoking parallels
between the Bible and football / Gary Graf.
        p. cm.
    Includes bibliographical references.
    ISBN 978-0-7648-1578-2
    1. Bible—Criticism, interpretation, etc.—Miscellanea. 2. Football—
Religious aspects—Christianity. 3. Football—History—Miscellanea. I.
Title.
    BS538.G62 2007
    242—dc22   2006103436

The editor and publisher gratefully acknowledge permission to reprint/
reproduce copyrighted works granted by the publishers/sources listed on page
181.

Liguori Publications, a nonprofit corporation, is an apostolate of the
Redemptorists. To learn more about the Redemptorists,
visit redemptorists.com.

Printed in the United States of America
15 14 13 12 11 / 5 4 3 2
First edition

CONTENTS

FOREWORD PASS

IF WE'RE TRULY MADE IN GOD'S IMAGE, then he must have a sense of humor, I've always believed. As evidence, I have often pointed to noses, ears, and giraffes...and the simple perfection of a smile. Something tells me that in the grand scheme of the universe, a bunch of grown men (make that overgrown men) chasing an inflated piece of pigskin around a field while throngs of face-painted fans cheer them on must be fairly humorous for the Almighty.

The Sabbath itself binds professional football and religion. Sunday is football's most holy day of the week, intertwining churches and champions, pastors and punters, flocks and fans.

Admit it...you've gone to early service to get home in time to change clothes and quickly park yourself in front of a big-screen TV, joining friends in watching your favorite team do battle with their division rival in the early Sunday game. Perhaps you've made a little steeple with your fingers as that second-year kicker prepared to wear the mantle of goat or hero depending on one touch of toe to leather. Maybe you have sent up a prayer of thanks after watching your team steal a victory in the final seconds of a game.

From Hail Mary passes to the Immaculate Reception, football has borrowed from Christianity. Stadiums are referred to as shrines. Legends like Vince Lombardi and Johnny Unitas take on iconic if not saintly status.

Is not a pregame tailgate party with the best of food and the best of friends the epitome of fellowship?

Football is practically its own religion in cities like Pittsburgh and Green Bay. It even has its own traditional hymns, such as the Rolling Stones' "Start Me Up" for kickoffs.

The connections cannot be denied. Neither can the fact that football remains a game, a pastime meant to bring joy and mirth.

A deft feel for the inherent joy and mirth in sports and religion makes Gary Graf's books so endearing. Graf applies lessons in Christianity with neither brimstone nor fire but rather with the gentle rub of glove oil into a mitt—as in *And God Said, Play Ball!*—or a gentle dab of eye black in *And God Said, It's Good!* Like a coach leading his players downfield, he kindly asks fellow Christians and sports fans to take a knee with him and outlines a play. But he's not calling for a slant pass or a run up the gut. Rather than calling in, "Red right switch split right two U corner halfback flat," Graf sends in, "Matthew 6:10."

Like any good coach, Graf gives his players—us fellow Christians and sports fans—a tap on the helmet, an arm around the shoulder, and a pat on the shoulder pads. He invites us to study up on the playbook that will lead us to lifelong victory...God's word.

KATHY SHELDON
Sporting News
April 2007

PRE-GAME SHOW

FOR A BOY WHO GREW UP THROWING, hitting, bouncing, catching, shooting, and kicking one shaped ball or another, the change of seasons was marked as much by the exchange of sports equipment as by the falling leaves or the blooming flowers. Fall meant football; winter, basketball; spring and summer, baseball. The sports pages were the only section of the paper worth reading. During the school year, homework was done against the background of Lon Simmons calling the play-by-play of the San Francisco 49ers, Bill King of the San Francisco Warriors and Oakland Raiders, and Lon Simmons and Russ Hodges doing the honors for the San Francisco Giants. My constant companions were larger than life: Hugh "The King" McElhenny of the 49ers, Nate "The Great" Thurmond of the Warriors, and Willie "Stretch" McCovey of the Giants. I collected baseball and football cards, and lived and died by my teams' performances.

My love of sports has accompanie°d me through the years, providing my dad and me at least one topic of conversation on the phone, just as it's given me something to chat about with my son as he masters the delicate timing required between clutch and gearshift. In fact, sports have been such a constant part of my life that I often view the world through its lens. Thus, associations between the games of my youth and pursuits of my life became inevitable.

One such pursuit has been my faith. As a Christian, I noticed similarities between the sport of baseball and Scripture. With a degree in math, I found it natural to make numerical connections. For instance, in the Bible there are four gospels to take you home to God. In baseball, there are four bases to take you home for a run. As an advertising copywriter, I have learned to look for associations between words. Thus, while the biblical phrase from Genesis, "...[to] cover it inside and out with pitch" (6:14), spoke of God's instructions to Noah for waterproofing the ark, it was also the first mention anywhere of pitching strategy. Beyond these simple musings came more profound relationships between the Bible and baseball, touching on themes of forgiveness, reconciliation, resurrection, and more. All of which led to the writing of *And God Said, "Play Ball!" Amusing and Thought-Provoking Parallels Between the Bible and Baseball.*

In that work I explored connections between the Good Book and great game through stories about Joseph of Egypt and Joseph of DiMaggio, the Book of Ruth and the book of Babe Ruth, Moses and Aaron (Hank, that is), Yogi, Jesus, and more. When I was writing *Play Ball,* I thought taking such an approach with the Bible and other sports might also prove fruitful, giving people a number of ways to deepen their faith through the games they loved. To be honest, it seemed a grandiose dream at the time. However, my editor at Liguori Publications, Paul Pennick, an avid Cardinals and Rams fan from the St. Louis area, also thought the idea had merit, especially given the response to our first collaboration together. He encouraged me to pursue a second project based on football.

And so, *And God Said, "It's Good!"* was born.

One of my earliest memories of football comes from my childhood. As a youngster of six, I couldn't wait until my dad got home to play catch on the patch of lawn in our front yard. I would run precise routes ending with lunging, diving, fingertip catches of tightly thrown spirals by my father. Of course, by routes I mean that I ran five yards from one side of the lawn to the other. In my mind's eye, no doubt, my dad's wobbly floaters have morphed into more tightly thrown balls over the years. I'm quite sure the lunging and diving portion of my description is accurate; my mom's complaints about grass stains on my jeans still ring in my ears. At that age, I'm just as certain there were many more misses than catches. Though my dad did his best to throw to my hands, that was no guarantee that the ball wouldn't go through my hands. Still, those early games of pass and catch inspired a devotion to football that has lasted to this day.

Growing up in Millbrae, California, our house was about fifteen miles from venerable Kezar Stadium on the edge of Golden Gate Park, early residence of the San Francisco 49ers. Put another way, our home was 26,400 yards from Kezar, a little less than half of the career passing total of Denver Broncos icon, John Elway. Being a Bay Area boy, it was only natural I became a member of the 49ers faithful. To my youthful way of thinking, if supporting one National Football League team was wonderful, then supporting two would be one plus wonderful. Thus, a few years later I also pledged my allegiance to Raider Nation. Now that I look back, I realize that to proclaim myself a fan of one team would surely be considered sacrilegious by fans of the other. But such was my fascination with the gridiron game.

Early suggestions that football and faith were intertwined came as a result of my father and my sister. My first football game came when I was ten years old. During the 1960 season, my dad took me to Kezar to see the hometown 49ers play the visiting Detroit Lions. Shades of Daniel being thrown into the lion's den. While the biblical prophet Daniel escaped unscathed, the 'Niners were not as fortunate, losing 24–0.

I had never before seen so many people gathered in one place. Even before the advent of the tailgate party, I was witness to the power of football—much like faith—at bringing a community together. Built in the 1920s, Kezar held a shade under sixty thousand people amid a single-tier of bleachers that circled the entire field. Its wood benches were hard and firm, all too similar to the pews at Saint Dunstan, the church of my youth. The brightly hued red-and-gold uniforms of the home team were reminiscent of colorful vestments used to celebrate Mass on special occasions. From coin toss to kickoff to silent signals by the referees, the game possessed a set of rituals that approximated those of the Mass.

While my first game provided hints that football and faith might be linked, an earlier episode with my sister Jacki left no question in my mind that one could discover lifesaving lessons in both. When I was still learning the game, I thought it would be wise for my sister to do the same. Thus, I took it upon myself to teach her how to punt. For some reason I thought it vital that she possess this particular skill at that point in her life. Of course, she was only three. In a prophetic vision of the domed stadiums that were to come twenty years later, I demonstrated the kick indoors. Putting, as well as punting, everything a six-year-old Junior 49ers could into it, I booted the pigskin a good twelve feet into the air. Unfortunately, her bedroom ceiling was only eight feet high. Not only that, there was a glass lampshade over the light bulbs in the middle of the ceiling. I say "was" because in short order the football smashed the light cover to smithereens, sending shards of glass raining down all over my sister.

Hearing the crash, my parents raced up the hallway to find my sister unharmed, sitting alone in the middle of the room with the football now in her lap. If you ask me, she looked as guilty as sin. At least she did from my vantage point hiding under her bed. Had it not been for Jacki silently pointing in my direction, I'm sure my parents never would have found me. The large paw of my father's hand dragged me out from beneath, despite my best efforts to grab anything in sight—frame, mattress, spread, blankets, sheets—that might delay the inevitable. Let's just say that for professing to be a football fan, my father seemed to be less than understanding of the situation.

Yet, I have to say that chain of events left an indelible impression on my mind. Good deeds deserved rewards; no bad deeds went unpunished. So even before being immersed in Christian teaching,

I had been introduced to the concept of good (and bad) works, as well as that of Judgment Day in the form of my punishment.

Despite having written *Play Ball*, I must confess that I was apprehensive about tackling its gridiron cousin. However, the night before I began putting words to computer screen I came across an item connecting faith to football, which provided me with just the impetus I needed to fully embrace the project. On May 3, 2006, Ben Maller posted the following on the Internet:

> Alabama football coach Mike Shula was a member of Campus Catholic church in Tuscaloosa but had to switch to another Catholic church in town after autograph hounds became too pushy, according to the Greg Larson radio show on WIOJ in Jacksonville Florida.[1]

To devout followers of the Crimson Tide, this probably didn't seem unusual. After all, in the years leading up to the 2005 season, the Tide had endured several mediocre if not dismal seasons by their high standards. So in leading Alabama to a 10–2 record that year, a Cotton Bowl victory over Texas Tech, and a final ranking of number eight nationally, Coach Shula may have been thought to walk on water. However, Mr. Maller concluded:

> The last straw was a guy standing at the end of the communion line with a football for Shula to sign.[2]

So outrageous was this story that none other than the pages of *Sports Illustrated* reported it in their section, "Sign of the Apocalypse."[3]

So there it was—a clear signal from the heavenly sideline. Just as if it was fourth down and inches, I was being instructed to go for it. All of which proved once again that God works in mysterious ways.

Now I must confess that I do not profess to be a biblical scholar, nor should this book be considered a theological treatise. Aside from neighborhood games of tackle football (from which my lower front tooth is still chipped) and games of touch football on the streets (from which I still have the scars), I have not suited up in any organized way. Rather than a scholar I consider myself a student of Scripture and sport. Always studying, ever learning. I hope this book inspires you to do the same.

For those who have read *And God Said, "Play Ball!"* some of what follows may seem similar. Certain biblical themes lend themselves to aspects that both baseball and football share. For those who are new to the *And God Said* series, welcome. The only thing I ask is that you don your favorite jersey, paint your face in the appropriate team colors, and get ready to rejoice. There's a lot to be learned about Hail Mary passes and answered prayers, Immaculate Receptions and Conceptions, biblical verses and double reverses, resurrections of careers and of lives, and more. You'll find that on any given Sunday we can all be brought closer to spirit and sport, faith and football, God and the gridiron. Enjoy!

CREATION:
THE BIG KICKOFF

ON SUNDAY, FEBRUARY 5, 2006, more than 141 million people in America gathered to worship. What makes this number all the more astounding is the fact these faithful were paying homage to the game of football.

Specifically, they had gathered around television sets all across the country to view parts, if not all, of Super Bowl XL, the ultimate contest of the 2005–2006 season between the Pittsburgh Steelers and the Seahawks of Seattle.

Pittsburgh was led by lantern-jawed coach Bill Cowher, folk hero Jerome "The Bus" Bettis, second-year quarterback "Big" Ben Roethlisberger, and multitalented wideouts, Antwaan Randle El and Hines Ward. Seattle's high-octane offense was powered by Pro-Bowl quarterback Matt Hasselbeck and league-leading rusher Shaun Alexander. Journalists wrote of Pittsburgh's quest for "one for the thumb," that is a fifth Super Bowl ring to go with their four other hard-earned pieces of championship jewelry. Seahawk coach Mike Holmgren was attempting to become the first coach to win Super Bowls with two different franchises, having accomplished step one of the process while leading the Green Bay Packers to the world title in the 1997 game, otherwise known as Super Bowl XXXI. There was also a good chance that this might be bruising running-back Bettis' last game, fittingly played in his hometown of Detroit.

By the time the scoreboard clock ticked down to 0:00, Pittsburgh had brought a fifth championship home to the Steel City with a 21–10 victory. And Super Bowl XL had set a record for television viewership surpassed only by the final episode of the long-running comedy *M*A*S*H*.

For those a tad rusty with their Latin, XL is Roman numeral for the number 40. However, it could just as easily stand for Xtra Large, as if to emphasize the outsized way football has captured the American consciousness. To give you some perspective, laid down head-to-toe, Super Bowl XL's total of 141.4 million viewers could circumnavigate the globe nearly six times.[1] Total viewership represented more people than voted in any presidential election ever. Now, one could argue that Coach Cowher had a better public approval rating than George W. Bush, but, even so, approximately 20 million more people watched the game than did their civic duty in the 2004 election. Should the viewers of XL ever decide to secede, the 141 million-plus people of Super Bowl nation would rank as the eighth most populous country in the world, just behind the 143.9 million citizens of Russia.[2] Need further proof of America's fascination with football? For the 2005–2006 campaign, the National Football League set a single season attendance record with nearly 21.8 million fans passing through stadium turnstiles.[3]

Football hasn't been the only institution posting positive gains among its followers. Not to be outdone, the Catholic Church in the United States had grown to more than 64 million people in 2004, as reported by Adherents.com.[4] For that same year, Adherents estimated that the number of Christians in America had surged to more than 224 million.[5]

Most population and cultural scientists would likely attribute such parallel growth purely to coincidence or a general trending upward in most populations overall. I would like to offer a counter hypothesis. I believe that football and faith are intertwined, connected to each other as inherently as a pass is between a quarterback and receiver. Further, I believe that by learning a little more about faith and football, we can all come to a deeper appreciation of both.

To understand the laces that bind football to faith, we have to go back to the beginning...of the game and of creation.

So, Sherman, set the Wayback machine for 1869. Usually, the boy Sherman of Peabody and Sherman fame from *The Bullwinkle Show* would man the controls. For our journey, I find it only fitting that Sherman Smith does the honors. After all, the Tennessee Titans running-back coach gained nearly 6,000 combined yards in an eight-year NFL career, mostly with the Seattle Seahawks.

By 1869, the War Between the States was over and baseball was in its infancy. Thanks to Rutgers and Princeton universities, another ball was to officially make its appearance in our country. And while round, it would soon take on a more pointed, elliptical shape over the years. On November 6, 1869, the two schools played the first college football game.[6] By football, I mean what we Americans call soccer.

Just as baseball was heavily influenced by the English games of cricket and rounders, the American sport of football similarly evolved from soccer and rugby. While soccer was the game first introduced on the college level, over the next seven years rugby gained favor among the major eastern schools. Seeing as though our Founding Fathers and early settlers sought independence from England, it was not surprising that our country sought freedom from English games. Thus, on November 23, 1876, representatives from the major colleges of the day—Harvard, Columbia, Princeton, and Yale—met at Massaoit House in Springfield, Massachusetts. It was here, at what was to be called the Massaoit Convention, that the first rules of American football were developed. Rugby Union rules were adopted in their entirety. One departure, however, concerned scoring. In rugby, a "touchdown" only counted toward the score if neither side kicked a "field goal." Princeton, Harvard, and Columbia agreed that four touchdowns would be worth one goal. Anyone worth his weight in kicking tees knows that in today's game a touchdown is worth twice as many points (6) as a field goal (3).[7] Obviously, the early versions of the game placed more store and score in the field goal, thus literally putting the "foot" in football.

Football made great strides in the '70s–'80s—the 1870s and 1880s. Walter Camp became Yale's first football coach in 1880. Under his leadership, a number of changes occurred that would Americanize football even more. Teams were reduced from fifteen players to eleven, the field was cut nearly in half, and the concept of the "scrimmage" was devised. At this line of scrimmage, a player heeled the ball backward to begin a game, the precursor to the center's hike of today. To minimize Princeton's and Yale's strategy to control the ball without trying to score, Camp introduced what is now called "change in possession."[8] A team had to surrender possession if they did not gain five yards after three "downs," that is, players brought down by being tackled. What's more, the coach introduced the seven-man offensive line, plus a quarterback, two halfbacks, and a fullback in the backfield. Not surprisingly, Mr. Camp is considered by many to be the Father of American Football.[9]

As for the birth of the National Football League, we have such evocative teams as the Panhandles, Triangles, Staleys, Maroons, Steam Roller, Steagles, and Bulldogs to thank, not to mention a Hupmobile showroom in Canton, Ohio.

In 1892, football entered into the ranks of wage-earning professions. In fact, Seattle Seahawks running back Shaun Alexander owes his newly signed $62 million contract to a former Yale All-American guard by the name of William Heffelfinger. That's right, Heffelfinger. Nicknamed Pudge, Heffelfinger wrapped all his fingers around $500 that year, becoming the first person to be paid to play the game of football, as a member of the Allegheny Athletic Association.[10] Four years later AAA, as they were known, also became the first team to field an entirely professional (meaning salaried) squad for a complete season. Of course, in Allegheny's case, the season was only two games long. But pro football had to start somewhere.

Other early highlights included the formation of a neighborhood team in Chicago, and baseball players tackling another sport. In 1899, the Morgan Athletic Club fielded a team. Originally called the Normals, the team changed its name to the Racine (for a street in the Windy City) Cardinals.[11] What makes this noteworthy is the team's nearly biblical lineage. The Normals begat the Racine Cardinals, which begat the Chicago Cardinals, who flew south to become the St. Louis Cardinals, who migrated west as the Phoenix Cardinals who have, at this point in time, finally landed as the Arizona Cardinals. While such peripatetic wanderings certainly aren't "Normal" for franchises, the Morgan Athletic Club-Racine-Chicago-St. Louis-Phoenix-Arizona Cardinals remain the oldest continuously operating team in pro football.

The NFL actually has baseball to thank for its name, if not its first baby steps. In 1902 baseball's Philadelphia Phillies and Philadelphia Athletics showed just how athletic they were. During the off-season, they formed football teams and joined the Pittsburgh Stars to form a pro football league named—cue the *Monday Night Football* musical fanfare—the National Football League. Seasonal highlights included the first night football game ever played, in which the Athletics prevailed 39–0 over the Kanaweola Athletic Club in Elmira, New York. Well-known A's pitcher Rube Waddell played football for the Athletics, while eventual baseball Hall of Fame pitcher, New York Giants Christy Mathewson, showed his toughness as a fullback for Pittsburgh.[12] Unfortunately, this incarnation of the NFL lasted but two seasons.

During the next ten years, a number of items of historical significance took place. In 1904, the value of a field goal was reduced from five points to four. That same year, halfback Charles Follis became the first known African American to play professional football, signing with the Shelby (Ohio) Athletic Club. In 1906, the forward pass was legalized, with the first authenticated completion coming between Massillon (Ohio) Tiger teammates George "Peggy" Parratt and Dan "Bullet" Riley.[13] Thus, the modern-day combos of Aikman-to-Irvin, Manning-to-Harrison, and Montana-to-Rice owe their fame and fortune to the pass completion between the unlikely named duo of Peggy-to-Bullet. In 1909, the field goal continued in its devaluation, dropping from four points to its current three. Rounding out our scoring summary, in 1912 the touchdown increased in value from five points to six.[14]

Two other noteworthy events took place in years to come. In 1913, Native American Jim Thorpe, a double gold medal winner in the Stockholm Olympics, agreed to play for the Pine Village Pros in Indiana. And in 1919, Earl (Curly) Lambeau and George Calhoun organized a team in Green Bay, Wisconsin. Lambeau's employer, the Indian Packing Company, provided money for equipment and allowed the team to use the company field for practices.[15] Thus, the Green Bay Packers were born to the delight of once and future Cheeseheads everywhere.

By 1920, pro football was in a state of upheaval due to rising salaries, players jumping from one team to another, and the use of college players still attending school. To arrive at rules that all teams would follow, an organizational meeting was held in Canton, Ohio, home of the powerhouse Canton Bulldogs. In addition to the Bulldogs, in attendance were representatives from the Akron Pros, the Cleveland Indians, and the Triangles of Dayton.

Adding to NFL lore was the location of this historic meeting: the Jordan and Hupmobile showroom in Canton. From 1909 until 1940 the Hupp Motor Company of Detroit produced half a million cars. The first police car used in Detroit was a 1910 Hupmobile, as were generals' staff cars in World War I.[16] In addition, the organization of professional football owes part of its foundations to the automaker that gave America the Roundabout and Torpedo.

A second meeting was held in Canton later in 1920 with representatives of teams from four states: Illinois (Decatur Staleys, Racine Cardinals, and Rock Island Independents), Indiana (Hammond Pros and Muncie Flyers), New York (Rochester Jeffersons), and Ohio (the four teams mentioned above). Out of this meeting, the American Professional Football Association (APFA) was born. Joining the league soon after were the Buffalo All-Americans, Chicago Tigers, Columbus (Ohio) Panhandles, and Detroit Heralds.[17]

In 1922 the APFA exchanged its initials for NFL, the National Football League. It should be mentioned that during that same year the Decatur Staleys (named after their owner) moved to Chicago, where they became known as the Chicago Staleys and then the (drum roll, please!) Chicago Bears. In 1925, five more franchises were added to the league, including the Detroit Panthers, Pottsville Maroons, Providence Steam Roller, and, lest we forget, a team from Manhattan called the New York Giants.[18]

By 1943, due to players going off to fight in World War II, the Steelers and Eagles were allowed to combine teams for one season. Known as Phil-Pitt, the team was affectionately called the Steagles by its fans. A year later, the Steelers and Cardinals merged for one year as Card-Pitt.[19] There is no indication that the name Stardinals caught on with press or public.

Over the years, the NFL's existence has been threatened by greed, fatalities, upstart leagues, World War II, upstart leagues, instability, and upstart leagues. More about this later, but suffice to say the League has prevailed to become by some accounts America's most popular sport. How did a game cobbled together from soccer and rugby achieve such heights? The answer may lie in the Bible.

Just as football has its father figures—from the Father of Football, Walter Camp, to Glenn "Pop" Warner to George "Papa Bear" Halas—we, too, have a father to guide us. Our Father, who art in heaven, is God almighty, ever-living creator of all that is. So awesome is the cosmos that early cultures developed creation stories to explain where we have come from and why we are here. One such tale is the first book of the Bible.

Genesis starts where all good stories do: In the beginning.

In the beginning when God created the heavens and the earth, the earth was a formless void and darkness covered the face of the deep, while a wind from God swept over the face of the waters. Then God said, "Let there be light"; and there was light. And God saw that the light was good; and God

*separated the light from the darkness. God called the light
Day, and the darkness he called Night. And there was evening
and there was morning, the first day* (Genesis 1:1–5).

As I explained in *And God Said, "Play Ball!"* for the next five days
God kept adding to his creation. On the second day came the oceans
and the sky. The third day brought about dry land and with it grass,
herbs, and fruit trees. By the end of the fourth day, God had created
the sun and moon. Upon closer examination, we find that days five,
six, and seven hold deeper meaning, at least as far as the game of
football is concerned. First, day five:

> *And God said, "Let the waters bring forth swarms of liv-
> ing creatures, and let birds fly above the earth across the
> dome of the sky." So God created the great sea monsters
> and every living creature that moves, of every kind, with
> which the waters swarm, and every winged bird of every
> kind. And God saw that it was good....*
>
> *And God said, "Let the earth bring forth living creatures
> of every kind: cattle and creeping things and wild animals
> of the earth of every kind." And it was so. God made the
> wild animals of the earth of every kind, and the cattle of
> every kind, and everything that creeps upon the ground of
> every kind. And God saw that it was good* (Genesis 1:20–21,
> 24–25).

Among the sea creatures that God created were Dolphins. Winged
birds included Cardinals and Falcons, Ravens and Eagles. Do you
detect a pattern here? Wild animals of the earth numbered Buffalo,
Panthers, Broncos, Colts, Jaguars, and Rams, not to mention Lions
and Bengals and Bears, oh my. Obviously, God had laid the groundwork for a good many NFL teams.

Day six revealed that:

> *...God created humankind in his image,*
> *in the image of God he created them;*
> *male and female he created them* (Genesis 1:27).

Think about it. Within humankind are represented Cowboys and Chiefs; Vikings and Buccaneers; Patriots and Texans; Giants and Saints. Far too many NFL team names to be considered mere happenstance.

Creation's culmination came, of course, on day seven:

> *And on the seventh day God finished the work that he had*
> *done, and he rested....So God blessed the seventh day and*
> *hallowed it, because on it God rested from all the work that*
> *he had done in creation* (Genesis 2:2–3).

Why did God rest on the seventh day? It couldn't have been because he was tired. God is abundant energy and boundless love. He doesn't get tired. It wasn't because he had nothing else to do. God is forever just as he is now, so he certainly knows what it's like to have time on his hands. Quite possibly the only reason he rested on the seventh day, which came to be called Sunday by the way, was so he could eventually watch football!

After all, did not God proclaim after each day's effort that it was good?

So, too, do play-by-play announcers exclaim, "It's good!" after key field goals kicked in crucial games. From New Orleans Tom Dempsey's NFL-record 63-yarder in 1970 against Detroit, to Jim O'Brien's clutch 32-yarder to give the Baltimore Colts a 16–13 victory over the Dallas Cowboys in Super Bowl V, from Garo Yepremian's 37-yard effort in December 1971 to give Miami the win over Kansas City in the longest NFL game ever played (82 minutes, 40 seconds) to Adam Vinatieri's 48-yard game-winner on the last play of Super

Bowl XXXVI, giving the New England Patriots a 20–17 victory over the St. Louis Rams, the call has been, "It's good!"

The kick is good. And God's creation, life itself, is good. From the birds of the air to the creatures of the deep to the beasts that walk the earth, it is good. Because we are made in God's image and likeness, whether we be Titans of business or construction workers, Giants in our field or college students, whether we be black, white, or Browns, whether we be youngsters or 49ers, whether we be men or women, sinners or Saints, we are especially good in God's eyes. Jesuit priest Michael E. Moynahan captured this thought quite eloquently in a prayer he wrote in which God speaks to us:

> ...I love you
> because I can't do
> anything else.
> I made you,
> every last part of you:
> all that's hidden
> and all that's revealed,
> all that's muddled
> And even all that's clear.
> You are,
> at the risk
> of repeating myself,
> dear to me.
> You are precious
> in my eyes
> because...
> just because
> you are mine.
> That's enough for me.
> And it will have to do
> for you.[20]

God rested on Sunday. Football is mostly played on Sunday. Co-incidence? I think not. God must have had football in mind when he created the heavens and the earth. How could this possibly be true? One explanation is so we could learn life lessons from both the Good Book and the playbook.

THE GOOD BOOK
AND THE PLAYBOOK I

FOOTBALL AND FAITH take much of their inspiration, and give us much of our learning, from their respective and respected volumes. Every college and pro team that dons helmets and pads has its own playbook, filled with complicated diagrams and esoteric language that would baffle the casual fan. Nickelbacks, dime packages, H-backs, stunts, red right 88, red right tight—spring right option. On the spiritual side, the Jewish and Christian faiths receive their instruction and guidance from the Good Book. For the followers of Judaism, that would be the Torah. For Catholics and Christians, of course, that refers to the holy Bible. For those who are unfamiliar with these collections of Scripture, the stories and lessons may also seem alien. However, with both books, the more they are studied, the more they enlighten.

As Saint Paul said in his Second Letter to Timothy:

All scripture is inspired by God, and is useful for teaching...and for training in righteousness, so that everyone who belongs to God may be proficient, equipped for every good work (3:16–17).

Scripture is given by the inspiration of God. It's for instruction so that all of us can be thoroughly equipped for every good work. Left unsaid, but certainly implied, is "every good work, including football."

Skeptical? Read on.

First, a quick tutorial of the Bible is in order. Think of it as an overview of a spiritual game plan. Divided into two main sections, the Good Book consists of the Old Testament and the New Testament. The first half (without a two-minute warning) is comprised of a number of the well-known stories of our youth. Genesis brings us the stories of Creation, Adam and Eve, Cain and Abel, Noah's Ark, Abraham and Isaac, Joseph and his coat of many colors, and more. Exodus recounts Moses leading the Israelites from captivity in Egypt. Adventures include the parting of the Sea of Reeds, encountering God as a burning bush, the receiving of the Ten Commandments, and the wanderings in the desert. Psalms represent a collection of 150 songs of praise, lament, and thanksgiving, reflecting the many facets of the Israelites' relationship with their creator. The books of the prophets, including Isaiah, Zechariah, and Daniel, tell of God's handpicked messengers bringing his word to a generally stubborn people.

Opening the second half are the four gospels of Matthew, Mark, Luke, and John. Each of these evangelists portrays the life of Jesus for their particular audience. For instance, Matthew's focus was to prove to Jewish readers that Jesus was the Messiah and promised king. In writing to Theophilus, a Gentile, Luke reassured his friend that Jesus' message of salvation was for Jews and Gentiles alike. Luke is also credited with a sequel of sorts, the Acts of the Apostles (think of it as Luke II), which, as its name suggests, recounts the triumphs and tribulations of the early followers of Christ. Much of the New Testament is taken up by epistles, letters primarily written by Paul and other leaders of the early Church encouraging new Christian communities that were forming around the Mediterranean area. Revelation is attributed to John of Patmos (a small island southwest of what is now Turkey). This last book of the Bible is his visionary account of the Judgment and Last Day. For many it's as difficult to clarify as explaining a double-reverse flea-flicker to a team of four-year-olds.

From all these writings, we learn how we first came into relationship with God, of his covenant with those who believe in him, of Jesus' instructions to us as how to live our lives, and how his death and resurrection have conquered sin and prepared the way for us to join in the kingdom of heaven.

We also learn a bit about the game of football.

"How awesome is this place!" (Genesis 28:17).

From the Book of Genesis comes the story of Jacob's well and Jacob's ladder. A bit of family history: God entered into covenant with Abraham, who had a son, Isaac. When the time came for Isaac to pass the family birthright to his descendant, eldest son Esau was first in line. However, Esau's younger brother Jacob gained the blessing through deception. Jacob's descendants became the twelve tribes of Israel. One night, while resting from his travels, Jacob lay down to sleep and had an amazing dream—angels were ascending and descending a ladder from the earth to the heavens. Upon waking, Jacob declared that the ground must be sacred because God dwelt there. "Awesome" describes the place of Jacob's ladder as well as one particular venue where football is played.

Lambeau Field.

As mentioned earlier, in 1919 Earl (Curly) Lambeau and George Calhoun organized the Green Bay Packers. At that time, many smaller towns in the Midwest had formed professional teams, and Green Bay, Wisconsin, was no exception. Immediately, the Pack was a success, going 10–1 in their first year of operation.[1] Three years later, though, the team had to withdraw from the APFA for using college-eligible players. Mr. Lambeau promised to obey league rules and used $50 of his own money to help buy back the franchise. Total cost: $250.[2] (Forbes.com estimated the Green Bay's franchise worth at $911 million in 2006![3]) Unfortunately, bad weather conspired with low attendance to hinder the team's financial success and Lambeau went broke.

Fortunately, the good news isn't just proclaimed in the gospels. It was also proclaimed in Green Bay. Local merchants arranged for the club to take out a $2,500 loan.[4] A public nonprofit corporation was established to operate the team with Curly Lambeau as the head coach and manager. Those merchants were indeed Packer Backers.

In 1957, the city dedicated a new stadium, a bowl-like structure, much like Kezar Stadium in San Francisco, seating 32,500.[5] In 1965, the field was rededicated as Lambeau Field in honor of the team's legendary first coach, who brought six of the teams' twelve championships to Green Bay.

Lambeau Field in Green Bay is truly awesome. Nowhere in America has a community embraced their pro football team or field with more loyalty. Games are regularly sold out. The waiting list for season tickets is thousands of names and decades of years long. Season tickets are bequeathed in wills. The community actually owns the team. Fans eschew more comfortable surroundings to bundle up in ski parkas and foam cheese hats to brave the winter elements as the home team does battle on, as Chris Berman of ESPN calls it, "the frozen tundra" of Lambeau Field.

And the fans have not gone unrewarded. Green Bay has a pack of championship trophies, twelve in all, more than any professional football team. Green Bay captured its first title in 1929 and its most recent in 1997. During the sixties, the Packers of Bart Starr, Paul Hornung, Jim Taylor, Ray Nitschke, and coach Vince Lombardi were no less than a dynasty, winning six championships in seven years, including the first two Super Bowls.

Today, Lambeau seats 72,922.[6] While that may not be surprising for a football stadium, consider this: the 2000 census placed Green Bay's population at 102,313. To put this in perspective, for Soldier Field to house an equal percentage of fans in Chicago, the Bears would have to increase capacity by nearly two million seats!

Lambeau Field is not the only awesome place to host the gridiron game. Fans of Soldier Field, Cowboy Stadium, and Arrowhead Stadium no doubt feel that their teams' homes deserve the same praise. Same with college football stadiums from the L. A. Coliseum to Michigan Stadium to Franklin Field in Philadelphia, all the way down to high-school fields and community center lawns used for Pop Warner football. Anywhere the game is played can be considered awesome just by the fact that fields allow football to be.

So it is with God. Quite naturally, one expects that the great cathedrals of the world from Saint Peter's in Rome to Saint Patrick's in New York, Notre Dame in Paris to Gaudi Cathedral in Barcelona, to be home to our Father. But the Almighty is present everywhere, be it the redwood forests in California, the Grand Canyon in Arizona, flowers in bloom, creatures of the deep, or the cosmos most far. Moreover, our Creator can also be found in our homes, our offices, our cars, with our loved ones, among strangers, or when we're alone. Realizing that we have the opportunity to encounter God wherever we happen to be, no wonder we exclaim, "How awesome is this place!"

"With an outstretched arm" (Exodus 6:6).

One of the greatest figures of the Old Testament was actually a murderer. Moses accidentally killed an Egyptian overseer who was beating a Jewish slave. Fleeing Egypt after his misdeed, Moses married and took up the life of a farmer. That is until God called upon him to lead his people out of Egypt. However, Moses couldn't fathom why he was chosen. In fact, he tried to talk his way out of the assignment:

"O my Lord, I have never been eloquent, neither in the past nor even now that you have spoken to your servant; but I am slow of speech and slow of tongue" (Exodus 4:10).

As you might have guessed, God wasn't buying it. Playing the role of speech coach, he instructed Moses to say,

> "Say therefore to the Israelites: 'I am the LORD; and I will free you from the burdens of the Egyptians and deliver you from slavery to them. I will redeem you with an outstretched arm....' " (Exodus 6:6).

Thus, not only did God lay the groundwork for the liberation of the Israelites, he also gave an indication of what football fans would see in Super Bowl X. In what many have called the most spectacular catch in Super Bowl history, Pittsburgh receiver Lynn Swann made a leaping, diving, falling, acrobatic catch of a Terry Bradshaw pass to help the Steelers defeat the Dallas Cowboys, 21–17. Swann caught four balls that day for 161 yards and a touchdown, but none was more dramatic than his redeeming Bradshaw's throw into tight coverage with an outstretched arm and incredible reception.[7] Making Swann's effort all that more remarkable was the fact that he almost didn't participate in the game, having suffered a severe concussion in the Steelers' previous playoff win against the Raiders.

God did not just offer his outstretched arm to the Israelites or only allow Lynn Swann to stretch out for a long pass. Our Father stretches his arm to each and every one of us in our times of gladness to rejoice with us, in our times of sadness to console us. It's as if he is reaching for us, stretching out to the utmost so that we might reach him. God loves us always and forever. Our task is to realize that we are so loved, and, in turn, offer such love to those around us, neighbors and strangers alike.

At this point in the "game," I am going to put to use one of my allocated time-outs. Just as announcers use lulls in their broadcast to often relive certain plays or achievements from the past, so too do I have a story to tell—a firsthand competitive encounter with Lynn Swann.

Swann attend Junipero Serra High School in San Mateo,

California. Named after the father of the California missions, Serra High was also later the home of New England quarterback Tom Brady, holder of three Super Bowl rings in four years. When Swann was a junior, he was part of a nearly unstoppable three-part offensive attack that also included quarterback Jesse Freitas and wide receiver Tom Scott. Freitas went on to play two seasons for the San Diego Chargers and Scott starred at the University of Washington, catching passes from Sonny Sixkiller, before playing in the Canadian Football League. All Swann did was become an All-American at the University of Southern California, a first-round draft choice, an All-Pro receiver for the Steelers, a Super Bowl Most Valuable Player, and a member of pro football's Hall of Fame.

Serra's nemesis in those years was Saint Ignatius High School in San Francisco, led by a quarterback by the name of Dan Fouts, the same Dan Fouts who gave wings to the Chargers of Don "Air" Coryell. A six-time Pro Bowl selection, Fouts passed for more than 40,000 yards in his Hall of Fame career. Needless to say, that was some kind of high-school football played in the Bay Area the late sixties.

My encounter with young Swann came in the summer of 1968. We had both attended an all-comers track meet held at San Mateo High School. I was not nearly the athlete that Lynn was. In addition to his football prowess, he was a starter on the Serra basketball team and won the state long jump title. For my part, I was fast enough to be on the track team, but not fast enough to excel.

At the all-comers meets, participants could sign up for as many events as they liked. This particular meet featured a triple jump competition. Having never done that, I thought I'd give it a try. Hop, skip, and a jump. How hard could it be? As it turned out, Swann and I jumped back to back. I powered down the runway, hit my mark, hopped, skipped, and jumped for all I was worth and...landed on the runway. I didn't even make it into the sand pit. Embarrassed, I then watched the graceful Swann take flight. He had more speed down the runway than I did, more power in his jumps, and more hang time in the air. He must have outjumped me by six feet or more. Which explains why Lynn Swann became an NFL star and I became someone writing about NFL stars.

Looking back, though, I realize that the episode had scriptural foundations. After all, each of us is given certain gifts, some to teach and preach, some to pass and catch, and some to relate faith and football together.

Now, back to the game and our God.

Following Exodus comes the Book of Leviticus, written primarily as instructions to the Jews as to how to live their lives in fellowship with God. In it we find a verse that speaks of respect.

You shall rise before the aged, and defer to the old; and you shall fear your God: I am the LORD *(19:32).*

To rise in the presence of an elder was a sign of respect. Likewise, the Jews were called to show reverence and obedience to God. Football also has its story of an elder and how an entire league and football nation looked up to him.

Naturally, I refer to George Blanda.

In a twenty-six-season, 340-game career, George Blanda became the inspiration to a younger and older generation. Competing in both the old AFL and NFL, he played until he was forty-eight years old. Let me repeat that. In a game of violent collisions, where helmets and pads are mandated for a player's safety, George Blanda performed until he was forty-eight years old! He was a veritable scoring machine, amassing 2,002 points from 236 touchdown passes, 9 rushing scores, 335 field goals, and 943 points after touchdowns. He even caught one pass in his career and intercepted another. Apparently to fight boredom, he even punted some.

However, what fans tend to remember most is one remarkable year when glorious George could do no wrong. During the 1970 season, Blanda was instrumental in delivering the Oakland Raiders from the jaws of defeat in five straight games. In a victory against the Steelers, Blanda took over for injured starting quarterback

Daryle Lamonica, threw for two touchdowns and added a field goal for extra measure. The next week his 48-yard field goal, with three seconds left in the game mind you, gained a 17–17 tie against the Kansas City Chiefs. Following that, in another relief appearance, he tossed a scoring pass and kicked a field goal in a win over the Cleveland Browns. While those heroics came with about ninety seconds remaining, all the time in the world comparatively speaking, his degree of field goal difficulty increased to 52 yards. Against the Broncos, Blanda relieved Lamonica in the fourth quarter just in time to throw another game-winning touchdown pass. Rounding out his fab five came a late field goal to defeat San Diego.[8] All this after being released in the preseason. All this at the age of forty-three.

I remember watching those games on television with my father. My dad, who was forty-nine at the time, became very interested in Blanda's efforts, and seemed to walk a little taller and smile a little wider with each weekly triumph. That's how it is with football and faith. All it takes is a particular game or player, gospel or passage, to spark an interest, to provide the gift that will elevate our spirits.

Written as poems to be sung in praise or lamented in sorrow, the Book of Psalms expresses the full range of human emotions. The 150 prayerful poems that comprise the book feature desperate cries of despair, confessions of wrongdoing, and joyful praise for God the creator, comforter and provider, as well as many reverential references to, believe it or not, football.

Is there a more glorious homage to right-handed quarterbacks anywhere than what is found in Psalm 98:1?

> *O sing to the LORD a new song,*
> *for he has done marvelous things.*
> *His right hand and his holy arm*
> *have gotten him victory.*

While the opening verse of Psalm 98 praises God for his help in guiding the Israelites from captivity in Egypt, it just as easily sings the praises of a number of field generals of the gridiron.

For starters, there's Sammy Baugh, who helped bring the modern passing game to football. In addition to helping the Washington Redskins win the NFL title in 1937, Slingin' Sammy led the league in passing six times, including 1943 when he finished first in passing, punting, and interceptions.[9] Not interceptions thrown by a quarterback, mind you, but passes intercepted as a defensive back! Talk about victories, Otto Graham directed the Cleveland Browns to ten division or league titles in ten years, including four straight with the All-America Football Conference and three in the NFL.[10] Bobby Layne put the roar in the Detroit Lions with three NFL titles in the 1950s.[11] Norm the "Dutchman" Van Brocklin teamed with Bob Waterfield in 1951 to bring the Rams their only title as residents of Los Angeles. As if to prove that was no fluke, the Dutchman guided the Philadelphia Eagles to the crown nine years later.[12]

One of the best-loved quarterbacks of all time was actually cut before throwing his first NFL pass. After being released by the Pittsburgh Steelers in 1955, Johnny Unitas signed with the Baltimore Colts a year later. And the rest, as they say, is hysteria. Playing in his ever-present black high-top cleats, Johnny U brought back-to-back championships to Baltimore in 1958 and 1959. In the '58 contest, the Colts were losing to the New York Giants, 17–14, with two minutes left to play. Starting at his team's own 14-yard line, Unitas calmly completed seven straight passes to set up the game-tying field goal with seven seconds left in regulation. Then in overtime, the Colts QB marched his team eighty yards, capping the drive with a handoff to Alan Ameche for the game-winning score.[13] Described by many as the "greatest game ever played," the OT thriller ushered pro football into the hearts and minds of the American public. To punctuate his career, Unitas also led the Colts to victory in Super Bowl V.

Any conversation about quarterbacks and ultimate victories would not be complete without mention of Aikman and Brady, Bradshaw and Montana. Troy Aikman helped the Dallas Cowboys claim three Super Bowls, as did Tom Brady (so far) for the New England Patriots. To date, no other QBs have won more Super Bowls than Terry Bradshaw and Joe Montana, each with four for the Pittsburgh Steelers and San Francisco 49ers respectively.

> *You have a mighty arm;*
> *strong is your hand* (Psalm 89:13).

The abovementioned verse again celebrates the power and justice of God almighty, as well as the prodigious numbers of certain strong-armed quarterbacks. Brett Favre brought the glory back to Green Bay with a Super Bowl victory in 1997. The Mississippi native has so far thrown for nearly 57,500 yards and 414 TDs. John Elway capped an illustrious career by winning back-to-back Super Bowls with the Denver Broncos. Known for his heroic come-from-behind victories, Elway amassed 51,475 yards and a neat 300 touchdowns. However, the title of Most Prolific Passer in NFL history goes to Miami Dolphins great, Dan Marino, passing for 61,361 yards over the course of his career, resulting in 420 touchdowns. That's nearly thirty-five miles of passing yardage!

Adding further validity to the connections between faith and football is this story about John Elway. Not only did he possess a strong arm, he was quite accurate with his throws. So much so, that the power of the passes would leave a mark on his receivers' chests. Caused by the tip of the football where its two seams intersected, the † shape of the bruise was called the Elway Cross.

An ode to creation, Psalm 104:19 recounts that God *made the moon* to mark the seasons, an obvious reference to Hall of Famer Warren Moon, who totaled more than 49,000 yards and 291 touchdown passes during his seventeen NFL seasons. For they did not win the land comes from Psalm 44:3. On one level it tells of how God denied the Egyptians victory over the Israelites. On another it summarizes every defensive stand in NFL history, the land in question being the ten yards required for a first down. While Psalm 147:9 praises God for his providence, it also refers to the victors of Super Bowl XXXV from Baltimore with the phrase, *and to the young ravens....*

PROVERBS, PROPHETS, AND PRO FOOTBALL

LEST YOU THINK that all football references in the Bible are about quarterbacks, let us turn to the Book of Proverbs. Again, some background. Israel's most famous king, David, from whose family Jesus descended, had a son, Solomon, also a king. Solomon was as wise as he was handsome. In a famous story from the First Book of Kings, the wisdom of Solomon is detailed.

Later, two women who were prostitutes came to the king and stood before him. The one woman said, "Please, my lord, this woman and I live in the same house; and I gave birth while she was in the house. Then on the third day after I gave birth, this woman also gave birth. We were together; there was no one else with us in the house, only the two of us were in the house. Then this woman's son died in the night, because she lay on him. She got up in the middle of the night and took my son from beside me while your servant slept. She laid him at her breast, and laid her dead son at my breast. When I rose in the morning to nurse my son, I saw that he was dead; but when I looked at him closely in the morning, clearly it was not the son I had borne." But the other woman said, "No, the living son is mine, and the dead son is yours." The first said, "No,

the dead son is yours, and the living son is mine." So they
argued before the king.

...So the king said, "Bring me a sword," and they
brought a sword before the king. The king said, "Divide
the living boy in two; then give half to the one and half to
the other." But the woman whose son was alive said to
the king—because compassion for her son burned within
her—"Please, my lord, give her the living boy; certainly do
not kill him!" The other said, "It shall be neither mine nor
yours; divide it." Then the king responded, "Give the first
woman the living boy; do not kill him. She is his mother."
All Israel heard of the judgment that the king had rendered;
and they stood in awe of the king, because they perceived that
the wisdom of God was in him, to execute justice (3:16–22,
24–28).

Solomon was not wise of his own accord. His wisdom came from
God, just as all our talents are gifts from above. This holds true
whether we have a slashing running style or musical talent, are
able to pass rush with speed and power or have a gift for medicine,
are able to accurately kick field goals from fifty yards or teach fifty
second-graders how to write.

As a side note, it should be mentioned that football, too, benefited
from the wisdom of Solomon—Freddie Solomon. Before 49ers Jerry
Rice and John Taylor were favorite targets of Joe Montana, there was
another pass-catching duo in town that helped bring home two Super
Bowl trophies to the city by the bay. While Dwight Clark provided
the possession receptions, Freddie Solomon stretched the defenses
with his speed and pass-catching ability. During his 49er career, he
totaled 329 receptions for nearly 5,000 yards, and 44 touchdowns.
While modest in some respects, those numbers add up to 15.8 yards
per catch, more than Rice averaged in his Hall of Fame career.

As far as the Book of Proverbs goes, many entries are attributed
to Solomon, some to other contributors. As the name of the book

suggests, Proverbs are sound bite-sized sayings of good advice, the wisdom of hard-earned experience handed down from our biblical elders. Like all Scripture, they are given to us so that we might learn how to better live our lives. And in one particular case, how we might learn about...you guessed it, football.

One of Solomon's early Proverbs provides guidance for the young:

> *Trust in the* LORD *with all your heart,*
>   *and do not rely on your own insight.*
> *In all your ways acknowledge him,*
>   *and he will make straight your paths....*
> *Then you will walk your way securely*
>   *and your foot will not stumble*
>   (Proverbs 3:5–6, 23).

There are two components to trusting God. One is to prayerfully discern his will for us in how we live our daily lives. Part of this comes from reflecting upon Scripture and the teachings of Jesus. Christ has given us all we need to know about living in right relationship to God—love our neighbors as ourselves. Anticipating our questions as to how to do that, Jesus provides us with those answers, too: feed the hungry, give drink to the thirsty, clothe the naked, visit the marginalized, comfort the afflicted, care for widows and orphans. From hurricane victims in New Orleans to earthquake victims in Pakistan, from sufferers of AIDs in Africa to refugees of war-torn Sudan, the world offers us plenty of opportunity to feed, clothe, and comfort those in need.

The second component to relying on the Almighty is to trust our God-given instinct. Call it conscience, the good angel whispering in your ear, that feeling in your gut, your heart's deepest desire, we have been given an internal moral compass on which to base our life's decisions. How often have we ignored that voice in our head or feeling in our heart to not drink and drive, to bite our tongue before lashing out, to give to the homeless instead of ignoring them, to become involved with our community instead of residing on the couch? That voice is the voice of God, that feeling is the life spark that our Creator placed inside each and every one of us, making us in his image and likeness. When we follow our instincts, more times than not, glorious things will happen.

Take Barry Sanders, for instance.

Not big for a running back, the five-foot eight-inch Sanders relied on explosiveness and catlike reflexes to stymie defenders. Before what many thought to be a premature retirement at the age of thirty-one, the Detroit Lion halfback had accumulated more than 15,000 yards rushing. Included in that total were five seasons of more than 1,500 yards, including 1997 when he ran for 2,053, becoming only the third player in NFL history to break the 2,000-yard mark. It wasn't just the number of yards Sanders gained that was amazing, it was how he did it. Often times he would run sideline to sideline to eek out a short gain. Other times he would squirt through a small hole and be gone. Most often, by virtue of his God-given talent and running instincts, he would start and stop, shift direction and gears, shimmy and spin, and be off to the races. Would-be tacklers were left literally grasping at air. Far from having his feet stumble, Barry Sanders ran safely to pay dirt ninety-nine times with another ten scores coming via the pass.

In a riddle meant to predict the coming of the Son of God, Proverbs 30:4 asks, in part, who has established all the ends of the earth? As we know, from mountain high to valley low, from sea to shining sea, God the creator has established the ends of the earth, and of the cosmos for that matter. He has also given us all the ends of the earth, as in the pass catching variety.

Just as the Almighty has blessed the earth with flowers and trees, birds and insects, animals and fish of all description, so has he done the same with football receivers. Tommy McDonald was only five-feet nine inches tall yet averaged a touchdown for every 5.9 receptions, playing mostly with Philadelphia. On the other extreme, at six-foot three, R. C. Owens of the 49ers had such great leaping ability that he popularized the "Alley-Oop" catch, where he out-jumped defenders for passes thrown intentionally high.

Don Hutson of the Green Bay Packers is considered the first modern superstar receiver. He created never-before-seen receiving routes such as the Z-out, buttonhook, and hook-and-go.[1] He also caught passes for the defense, totaling 30 interceptions in his career.

Hall of Famers Raymond Berry of the Colts and Steve Largent of the Seahawks made their reputations as precise route-runners with sure hands. Not gifted with great speed, Berry compensated with hard work and guile. By his own count, he had developed eighty-eight different moves to get open.[2] Largent was thought to be too small and too slow to play in the NFL, so the Oilers traded him to the Seahawks—for an eighth-round draft choice. Largent "only" lasted fourteen years in the league, accumulating 819 receptions and 100 touchdowns.

For years, the tight end position was thought of as just another blocker on the offensive line. That is until Baltimore Colts John Mackey brought speed to the position. Not only did Mackey have the wheels for 331 catches and 5,236 yards during his career, in his rookie year he averaged 30.1 yards in kickoff returns. That's right, kickoff returns. If Mackey redefined the tight end position, Ozzie Newsome revolutionized it. The Wizard of Oz turned the tight end into a viable offensive scoring option, with 662 grabs for nearly 8,000 yards and 47 trips to the end zone. Current Kansas City Chief Tony Gonzalez surpassed Ozzie's Hall of Fame numbers with his own combination of size and speed. Tony G. has totaled 721 catches, 8,710 yards, and 61 scores with plenty of fuel still left in the tank.

Cris Carter and Tim Brown made careers out of being possession receivers, those wideouts who consistently keep drives alive with their ability to get open and hold on to the ball. Each player caught over 1,000 passes. Brown, playing primarily for the Raiders, grabbed 1,094 balls for 14,934 yards; Carter, splitting his career for the most part between the Minnesota Vikings and Philadelphia Eagles, caught 1,101 passes for 13,899 yards.

Then there are the wonderfully athletic receivers who combine speed, great leaping ability, sure hands, and acrobatic grace. James Lofton became the first receiver to snare touchdown passes in the seventies, eighties, and nineties en route to 764 catches covering 14,004 yards in his career. Playing for the Browns and Dolphins, Paul Warfield averaged 20.1 yards per catch in his career, meaning any time his quarterback tossed him the ball Warfield would gain, on average, enough yardage for two first downs. With more than 10,000 yards in receiving already, Randy Moss has made the spectacular catch seem almost ordinary, while Marvin Harrison is putting up Hall of Fame numbers with the Colts: 1,022 receptions, 13,697 yards, and 122 TDs.

Then there is the incomparable Jerry Rice. Known for his hard work and soft hands, Rice's preseason workouts were as grueling as they were legendary. Many a teammate tried to keep up, especially running The Hill, only to be left gasping for air or losing their lunch. Rice not so much rewrote the record book as he took possession of it. Most career receptions (1,549), most career receiving yardage (22,895), most career touchdowns (207), most consecutive games with at least one reception (274), the list goes on and on...and on and on. Add to that three Super Bowl rings while with the 49ers and one Super Bowl MVP.

From Lance Alworth to Joe Zelenka, God gave us all the ends of the earth. But he also has provided us with all the doctors of the earth, all the teachers, software developers, social workers, police officers, accountants, carpenters, bakers, engineers, nurses, custodians, merchants, mechanics, and more. Simply put, all that we have, and all that we are, are gifts from God.

If ever there were two books in the Old Testament that spoke to the sport of football and the Spirit within us, they would be Ecclesiastes and Daniel. Many scholars attribute the Book of Ecclesiastes to Solomon. Like his father before him, Solomon stumbled following

God's path. Father David sent one of his military leaders to sure death on the battlefield so he could bed the man's wife, Bathsheba. Son Solomon took to idolatry and the pursuit of foreign wives. Upon repenting, the wise king authored Ecclesiastes as a way to find meaning from life, primarily his exhortation to be in awe of God and to respect his laws for we will all be judged on the Last Day. Showing wisdom beyond his years, and millennia ahead of the Super Bowl, Solomon also made several references to football.

The third chapter of Ecclesiastes is one of the most well-known portions of the Bible, even if people may not realize it. This is due for the most part to the song-writing talents of Pete Seeger and a remarkable recording of his song "Turn! Turn! Turn!" by The Byrds in the 1960s. Scripture and song both speak to sport.

For everything there is a season (Ecclesiastes 3:1).

There is a time in our lives for all things. A time to be born, a time to die, a time to weep, a time to laugh. What's more, there is a time for God in all these things. Saint Ignatius of Loyola realized this hundreds of years ago.

Ignatius was a man of adventure in sixteenth-century Spain, chivalrous, all about fighting for the king and ladies of the court. That is until he almost lost a leg to a cannonball. During his recuperation from his battlefield injury, Ignatius read a book on the saints. Captivated by the way they led their lives, this small man from Loyola decided to devote himself to God instead of the king. In time, he founded the Society of Jesus, later to be called the Jesuit Order, and wrote his own book about spiritual exercises. All of which is by way of introducing his concept of consolation and desolation.

Ignatius came to believe that whether we have moments of joy or sadness, grief or consolation, any and all are opportunities to find God. The birth of a child, the beauty of nature, a homeless man on the street, the loss of a loved one, a punt return for a touchdown. The death and devastation left behind by Hurricane Katrina allowed thousands of people in the rest of country to open their hearts to help their fellow Americans. The tranquillity and humility of the Dali Lama gives those who come in contact with him a feeling of the sacred, of being loved unconditionally. In short, God is present in all people, places, and events. We just have to be willing to find him. Or let him find us.

Beyond the obvious fall and winter football schedule, there is also a season to each player's career. Springtime represents nurturing and development. So it was when the Cincinnati Bengals drafted USC quarterback Carson Palmer in 2003, then let him learn the game from the bench for a season before turning the reins of the team over to him. The wait was worth it as Palmer led the team to the playoffs in 2005, ending a drought of fifteen seasons. Summer is the prime of a player's career. Witness Colts QB Peyton Manning with his recent streak of six 4,000-yard seasons, and his record 49 touchdown passes thrown in 2004. Autumn brings the fall of leaves and a player's production. After eleven seasons with at least 50 receptions as a starter for the Raiders, wideout Tim Brown ended his career as a player off the Buccaneer's bench, starting only four games and catching only 24 balls. Winter with its bare trees and dark nights is analogous to the end of a career, either by retirement, injury, or diminishing talent. For most players, it's a dark time.

Our lives are not much different. As youngsters we learn about life and love. In middle age, we start families of our own and achieve success in our professions. In our fifties or sixties, we may experience a decline in health or be affected by downsizing at the office. In our later years, we experience the loss of contemporaries, our spouse, and eventually all are called home to our Creator. Yet, through each of our seasons, as Saint Ignatius taught us, we can find God.

> [A] time to seek, and a time to lose;
> a time to keep, and a time to throw away
>   (Ecclesiastes 3:6).

Solomon sums up quite nicely the ebb and flow of football seasons and lives. Any running back who has ever strapped on a helmet knows all about seeking and losing yardage. A bobbled exchange, a slip of the foot, a plugged hole, a blitzing linebacker can all cause even the shiftiest of running backs to lose a yard or more. Fortunately, most rushing attempts afford opportunities to gain back what was lost and then some.

Franchises gain and lose as well. In 1976, Tampa Bay started its existence by losing its first twenty-six games. All of the frustration and ineptitude seemed to pay off when the Buccaneers captured the flag by winning Super Bowl XXXVII after the 2002 season. Baltimore lost its entire team when the Colts moved to Indianapolis for the 1984 season, only to gain a franchise when the erstwhile Cleveland Browns became the Ravens of Baltimore twelve years later. Not to be outdone, Cleveland resurrected its beloved Browns via an expansion team in 1999.

Quarterbacks everywhere take to heart the second half of the above verse from Ecclesiastes. Under a severe rush, a QB must make split-second decisions, reading his receivers' routes, judging the tightness of coverage, estimating the defenders' imminent arrival, gauging his linemen's protection. Should his wideouts be covered and his own escape precarious, he must either throw the ball out of bounds to pass another day or keep and protect the ball from the oncoming rushers.

We, too, have a time to keep and a time to throw away. In the early years of our adult lives, it's all too easy to become wrapped up in material things. We buy homes, cars, big screen TVs, stereos, suits, shoes, boats, skis, cameras, cell phones, time shares, golf clubs, season tickets, you name it. With maturity, we realize that never-ending spending is not the way to happiness. For those who have much, it is our duty to help those who have little. Perhaps we donate some of our clothes and belongings to charity. Maybe we donate some of our time to a worthwhile cause such as the local homeless shelter or Big Brothers or Sisters. Football or life, there is a time to keep and a time to let go.

Confidante to Babylonian King Nebuchadnezzar and Perisan ruler Cyrus, Daniel wrote his book to encourage Israelites that, even though they had been held captive in Babylonia, God would restore and reward his chosen ones. Written in the fifth century before Christ, the Book of Daniel also predicted the coming of several members of the National Football League.

Thrown into a den of lions (6:7).

Those familiar with the story of Daniel know that he was cast into a den of lions for being true to the one true God. One growling beast after another left him unharmed. This was not the case with football teams visiting Detroit, especially in the 1950s. Behind QB Bobby Layne and running back Doak Walker on offense and middle linebacker Joe Schmidt on defense, the Lions won four division titles during the decade, as well as back-to-back NFL championships in 1952 and 1953, and another league title four years later.

In his seventh chapter, Daniel tells of a dream in which various animals represent oppressing empires of the Jews, thought to be the Babylonians, Medo-Persians, Greeks, and Romans. He also foretells of the coming of a number of NFL franchises:

> [A]nd four great beasts came up out of the sea....The first was like a lion and had eagles' wings....Another beast appeared, a second one, that looked like a bear....After this, as I watched, another appeared, like a leopard [a Bengal, Jaguar, or Panther perhaps?]....After this I saw in the visions by night a fourth beast [quite possibly a reference to Buffalo], terrifying and dreadful and exceedingly strong (7:3–7).

If Daniel had lived in the twenty-first century, the animals in his visions may have referred to Iraq and Iran, Sudan and the Congo, Korea and Columbia, Israel and Palestine, any place where violence and oppression keep the world a broken place. With his mentions of lions and eagles and bears, the prophet must have known that our planet can learn a lesson from football. Take in a game and you'll see two teams push and shove, hit and tackle one another in a grueling fight over territory. But when the final gun goes off, combatants shake one another's hands, offer words of encouragement and consolation, and embrace in respect. If only the world could too.

In between the books of Ecclesiastes and Daniel falls the Book of Isaiah, the ninth chapter of which offers an opportunity that allows us to know Jesus and the game a little better.

An advisor to four kings of Judah, Isaiah exhorted the Israelites to mend their wicked ways or face disastrous consequences. At the same time, Isaiah spoke of promise and hope, predicting that one day a Messiah would bring comfort and joy to the chosen people.

> *For a child has been born for us,*
>   *a son given to us;*
> *authority rests upon his shoulders;*
>   *and he is named*
> *Wonderful Counselor, Mighty God,*
>   *Everlasting Father, Prince of Peace* (9:6).

Sound familiar? Composer George Handel used this verse from Isaiah as the basis for the lyrics to his world-famous oratorio *Messiah*, a line of which also refers to a number of football players who have had titles bestowed on them as a way for people to better relate to them as players and people.

And he is named: Bam and Bambi, Boomer, Bruiser, Bronko, Bulldog, Buck and Bullet; The Assassin, The Snake, The Toe and The Bus; Red, Ace, Dutch, Link, Tank and Turk; Broadway Joe and Leo the Lion; Prime Time and Night Train; Peggy and Pudge; L.T. and T.O.; The Golden Boy and The Galloping Ghost; The Mad Bomber and The Mad Stork; Mercury and Hollywood, Dandy, Deacon, and Crazy Legs; Curly and Tuffy; and last but not least, Fudgehammer.

Even teams have their own monikers: The Orange Crush, Purple People Eaters, Fearsome Foursome, Steel Curtain, and Monsters of the Midway.

Nicknames offer us an insight into a player's youth. They remove players from the pedestal and make them more accessible in our minds. Nicknames help keep the game young, reminding us that even if grown men are playing, football is still also a boys' game, from Pop Warner youngsters to high-schoolers. Likewise, when we speak of God, it is hard for us to imagine a relationship with the all-powerful, ever-living creator of all that is. So in our human way, we bestow "nicknames" on God himself. He becomes more knowable and approachable to us. When we pray to our Father, we in effect become children of God. When we refer to Jesus as the Savior of the world, we become the rescued.

Whether we read about Creation stories, Noah's Ark, Joseph and his coat of many colors, or adventures of escape from Egyptian soldiers by the parting of the sea, we are being taught of God's covenant with us. When we sing the Psalms, recite the Proverbs, or read the Song of Solomon, we learn what it is to praise God, thank God, petition God, place our troubles before God. Similarly, the more we understand the personalities, procedures, and plays of the game, the more we appreciate football. Remarkably, the more we study the one helps us appreciate the other...and vice versa.

THE GOOD BOOK
AND THE PLAYBOOK II

IN THE NEW TESTAMENT, evangelists Matthew, Mark, Luke, and John spread the Good News, that is, the Word made flesh, the Son of God, Jesus Christ. We learn of Christ's birth, life, teachings, miracles, parables, passion, death, and resurrection. Themes occur time and again, instructing us on the value and power of forgiveness, service, prayer, reconciliation, and love. With so much going on in the gospels and epistles, it's no wonder biblical scholars have devoted so little time to the good news of the gridiron.

"For we observed his star at its rising, and have come to pay him homage" (Matthew 2:2).

Early in Matthew's Gospel come tales of intrigue. After establishing that Jesus came from the House of David, as was predicted in the Old Testament, and telling of his birth by a virgin, fulfilling the prophecy from Isaiah 7:14, Matthew tells about the three wise men journeying from the east to pay homage to the newborn king. When the Roman governor of Palestine, King Herod, heard word of the birth, he attempted to have the Magi tell of the infant's whereabouts. Ostensibly this was so Herod could pay his respects. However, after presenting the baby Jesus

THE GOOD BOOK AND THE PLAYBOOK II

with gifts of gold, frankincense, and myrrh, the wise men were warned in a dream to avoid Herod for he planned to destroy Mary and Joseph's child.

Not only did a star lead the wise men to find Jesus, a Starr led a storied franchise to the Promised Land of the NFL championship. Though his career statistics are modest (24,718 yards and 152 touchdown passes), especially in light of today's modern passers, Bart Starr shown bright when it came to guiding his team to victory. In the span of eight seasons, he directed the Green Bay Packers to six division crowns, five NFL championships, and victories in the first two Super Bowls ever played. Along the way he earned an MVP award as well as two MVPs in the Super Bowl. Not bad for a seventeenth-round draft choice. No wonder fans from the East and West, and players from the NFL and AFL, came to "worship" him.

In the fifth chapter of Matthew's Gospel, the evangelist recounts Jesus' explanation regarding the letter and spirit of the law. In so doing, Christ provided affirmation of the accuracy of Scripture, as well as mentioned one of the most famous quarterbacks in New York Giant history.

> "Do not think that I have come to abolish the law or the prophets; I have come not to abolish but to fulfill. For truly I tell you, until heaven and earth pass away, not one letter, not one stroke of a letter, will pass from the law until all is accomplished" (5:17–18).

"Letter and stroke of a letter" have also been translated as "jot and tittle." A *jot* is the least part of something, while a *tittle* is a small punctuation mark, an iota, or a New York Giants quarterback.

Yelberton Abraham Tittle presided over the Giants from 1961 through 1964. Coming from the 49ers in a trade, Y. A. took over the QB reins from popular Charlie Conerly, and promptly continued the Giants' winning ways. Y. A.'s last name could just as easily have been Title, for he led New York to three straight division crowns beginning in his first season with the team. Over his NFL career, he passed for more than 28,000 yards, passed and rushed for 245 TDs, made seven Pro Bowls, and was named NFL MVP twice. However, the most enduring image of this Hall of Famer is kneeling battered on the field of battle, helmet off, blood streaming down the side of his face, emblematic of the competitor he was.

The word *tittle* is little used in this day and age. That the Bible and the NFL record books both have reference to a "tittle" goes beyond coincidence to the connection that both faith and football have. As if to add even further evidence to the intertwining of the two, the Giants quarterback's middle name, Abraham, is that of one of the central characters of the Old Testament, with whom God made the covenant with the Jews, precursors to Christ's covenant with humanity.

As for the Gospel according to Luke, little doubt exists over his reference to the 1982 NFC championship playoff game between the Dallas Cowboys and San Francisco 49ers:

> When [Jesus] *had finished speaking, he said to Simon, "Put out into deep water and let down your nets for a catch." Simon answered, "Master, we have worked all night long but have caught nothing. Yet if you say so, I will let down the nets." When they had done this, they caught so many fish that their nets were beginning to break. So they signaled their partners in the other boat to come and help them. And they came and filled both boats, so that they began to sink....[A]ll who were with him were amazed at the catch...* (5:4–7, 9).

The Catch. In San Francisco 49ers history, any fan to ever wear the red and gold knows where they were on January 10, 1982, at the moment of The Catch. (I was in Studio City, California, at a friend's house watching the game on television.) In a seesaw battle, the Cowboys had taken a 27–21 lead with time running down in the fourth quarter. San Francisco quarterback Joe Montana proceeded to lead his team down to the Cowboy six-yard line with fifty-eight seconds to go. Third down. In a play designed for wideout Freddie Solomon, Montana found his primary receiver covered. Under a fierce rush from Dallas defenders Ed "Too Tall" Jones, Larry Bethea and D. D. Lewis, Montana was forced to backpedal to buy time. Just when it looked like he would be dumped for a sack or forced out of bounds, the Niner QB threw high to the back of the end zone. Dwight Clark, all six feet four inches tall of him, leaped as high as he could, grasping the ball by the very tips of his fingernails at the very last moment before it sailed away.[1] It's good! Touchdown 49ers! San Francisco went on to win the game, 28–27, and two weeks later captured their first of five Super Bowl trophies. Truly, Dwight, Joe, every 49er and Cowboy, those in attendance and those watching on TV were amazed at The Catch.

Looking back, the only question remains: Did Luke first write about The Catch to foretell football lore nearly two thousand years in the future? Or did he write his gospel story so that football fans of the twenty-first century would learn about one of Jesus' miracles?

I believe the answer is yes.

One of Jesus' most famous and poetic parables comes from John's Gospel. In it, we learn that apart from Christ, our spiritual lives will wither and die. Conversely, through the Son of God, we are able to accomplish great things.

> *"I am the vine, you are the branches. Those who abide in me, and I in them bear much fruit, because apart from me you can do nothing. Whoever does not abide in me is thrown away like a branch and withers; such branches are gathered, thrown into the fire, and burned. If you abide in me, and my words abide in you, ask for whatever you wish, and it will be done for you. My Father is glorified by this, that you bear much fruit and become my disciples"* (15:5–8).

This parable also points out a veritable truth concerning football. Teams will only bear fruit by abiding in, and working with, one another. Certainly this is true with quarterbacks and receivers. They must be on the same page of the playbook. A quarterback must learn his wideout's routes, speed, and leaping ability. A wideout must adjust to his quarterback's arm strength, touch, and the spiral he puts on the ball. When all works well, Branches indeed produce a great deal.

Take Cliff and Deion, for instance.

During a seven-year period from 1977 to 1984, the Oakland/L.A. Raiders claimed three Super Bowls, with Cliff Branch providing the deep threat for quarterbacks Ken Stabler and Jim Plunkett. In those games, Raider Branch caught 14 passes for 176 yards and 3 touchdowns. Patriot Branch was even more fruitful. In Super Bowls XXXVIII and XXXIX, he proved to be New England QB Tom Brady's favorite target. Deion Branch caught a combined 21 passes, a Super Bowl record, for 276 yards and a score. His eleven grabs in the 2005 championship game tied another record.

[T]he rush of a violent wind (Acts of the Apostles 2:2).

A good deal of what we know of the early Church comes from the Acts of the Apostles. This portion of the New Testament, written by the evangelist Luke, recounts the words and actions of Christ's followers after his death and resurrection. In this case, the rushing wind refers to the Holy Spirit coming to the disciples on Pentecost.

> *When the day of Pentecost had come, they were all together in one place. And suddenly from heaven there came a sound like the rush of a violent wind, and it filled the entire house where they were sitting. Divided tongues, as of fire, appeared among them, and a tongue rested on each of them. All of them were filled with the Holy Spirit and began to*

speak with other languages, as the Spirit gave them ability (2:1–4).

As a child, receiving my Catholic education at St. Dunstan School, I first learned of the Blessed Trinity expressed this way: Father, Son, and Holy Ghost. Years later, the Holy Ghost was referred to as the Holy Spirit, perhaps in an effort to dispel notions in young, impressionable minds of the Spirit somehow being related to Casper, the Friendly Ghost. Looking back, one reason for the original Holy Ghost language may have had to do with football.

In 1925, a rushing violent wind had also descended upon the gridiron. A mortal, he too was a ghost, of the galloping variety. Red Grange was so elusive a runner, stopping him was like attempting to grab the wind, like trying to tackle a ghost. As the Holy Ghost illuminated the disciples regarding the Word of God, the Galloping Ghost enlightened the country concerning the wonders of the game.

Bears owner George Halas signed Harold Edward Grange directly out of the University of Illinois as a way to entice college fans to the professional version of the sport. So successful was this endeavor in Chicago, that Papa Bear and the Ghost took the show on the road. During a sixty-seven–day tour, the Bears played nineteen games all around the country, including a game against the New York Giants in the Polo Grounds. That the Bears won that contest 19–7 is incidental. What mattered most is that nearly 70,000 people attended, helping to save the financially strapped Giants franchise.[2] While Grange's numbers cannot compare to other, future Hall of Famers, the Ghost has been credited for popularizing professional football in the eyes of fans everywhere. Just as the Holy Ghost, or Spirit, allowed the disciples to spread the Good News of the Lord.

Now there were devout Jews from every nation under heaven living in Jerusalem. And at this sound the crowd gathered and was bewildered, because each one heard them speaking in the native language of each. Amazed and astonished, they asked, "Are not all these who are speaking Galileans? And how is it that we hear, each of us, in our own native language? Parthians, Medes, Elamites, and residents of Mesopotamia, Judea and Cappadocia, Pontus and Asia, Phrygia and Pamphylia, Egypt and the parts of Libya belonging to Cyrene, and visitors from Rome, both Jews and proselytes, Cretans and Arabs—in our own languages we hear them speaking about God's deeds of power." All were amazed and perplexed, saying to one another, "What does this mean?" (Acts of the Apostles 2:5–12).

What does this mean!?! Looking back, one could very easily conclude that the Word of God is meant to be heard by people of all nations. However, to paraphrase Luke, one might reach a similar conclusion regarding the gridiron game.

"Are not all these who play football? And how is it that we cheer, each in our own language those players from where we live? Bills, Bengals, Browns, and Broncos; Chiefs and Cowboys; Giants and Saints; Cardinals, Falcons, Ravens and Eagles; Titans and Texans; Rams and Raiders; those dwelling in Green Bay and Tampa Bay, San Diego and San Francisco; New York and New England, Minnesota and Miami; Pittsburgh and Seattle, Jacksonville and Indianapolis, Carolina and the parts of DC at the corner of Independence Avenue and 22nd Street, visitors and home teams, both whites and blacks, Samoans and Hispanics, we see them playing our own game as a wonderful work of God."

Football brings together people of different religions, races, nationalities, and upbringings, molding them into thriving communities where all work together to serve one another toward a common goal and goal line. Leave it to the game to be a microcosm of the potential God sees for all of humanity.

So Moses...was powerful in his words and deeds (Acts of the Apostles 7:22).

In this section of Acts, Luke recounts God's relationship with Moses and how the latter led the Israelites out of captivity from Egypt. It turned out that not only was Moses mighty in words and deeds, but so too was Joe Namath.

The term "Super Bowl" first appeared in reference to the third NFL-AFL championship game, between the NFL's Baltimore Colts and the upstart New York Jets of the American Football League. Subsequently, all league championship games were referred to as Super Bowls. Even the first two NFL-AFL title games, won by the Green Bay Packers, were called Super Bowls retroactively.

Going into Super Bowl III, the Baltimore Colts were favored by as many as twenty points. And why not. They finished the regular season 13–1, shut out Cleveland in their NFL playoff game, 34–0, and had such stars as league MVP Earl Morrall at quarterback, receivers Jimmy Orr and John Mackey, running back Tom Matte, middle linebacker Mike Curtis, and defensive lineman Bubba Smith (prior to his fame as a spokesman for Miller Lite beer). As for the Jets, quarterback Joe Namath completed fewer than 50 percent of his passes for the regular season. Hardly an awe-inspiring number.

Still, prior to the game, Broadway Joe guaranteed a Jets' victory. Then, he backed up his words with mighty deeds. Namath completed 17 of 28 passes for 206 yards in winning the Super Bowl MVP award and, more importantly, masterminding perhaps the biggest upset in Super Bowl history. Final score: Jets 16–Colts 7.

Two epistles pick up the theme of teamwork explored above between quarterbacks and receivers. The first comes by way of the letter to the Romans from Saint Paul. That's Saint Paul, the disciple, not Saint Paul, the Ideals, a Minnesota team that participated in the first game ever played by a member of the newly formed American Professional Football Association. On September 26, 1920, those

Ideals were crushed by APFA member Rock Island Independents, 48–0.[3] Fortunately, the ideals of Saint Paul, the man, have been of stronger stuff.

Originally Paul was called Saul and thought nothing of persecuting the Jews. Of course, being struck down by Christ on the road to Damascus can cause a guy to rethink his priorities. Saul became Paul, one of the most dedicated advocates of the Word the world has ever known. Over four journeys, Paul traveled to Antioch, Cyprus, the cities of Galatia in Asia Minor, Macedonia, and present-day Greece, Ephesus, Jerusalem, Crete, Rome, and more. Talk about a road trip. In the course of his establishing Christian communities in these locales, he often had to send letters to instruct or clarify, admonish or support, the fledgling "churches." Those letters are Paul's epistles.

We know that all things work together for good for those who love God, who are called according to his purpose (Romans 8:28).

Paul wrote of all the good that can be done if we but do God's will, if we just follow his path for us. The disciple also spoke of the value of playing, as well as praying, together.

Every player on a football team has a purpose, from offensive linemen who open up holes for running backs and protect quarterbacks to defensive backs who form the last line of defense. Those who consistently perform their assigned tasks to the best of their ability, and who work together for the good of the team, meet with success.

Just as John described in his second epistle.

Be on your guard, so that you do not lose what we have worked for, but may receive a full reward (2 John 8).

As the evangelist suggests, teams work together for a common goal in hopes of being rewarded with a Super Bowl championship. Recently, the New England Patriots have embodied the team concept, resulting in three Super Bowls in four years. Tom Brady utilizes all his weapons on offense, allowing each teammate to make full use of his skills. On the other side of the ball, the defense executes its schemes well, with each player backing up his com-Patriot. Their approach can be summed up simply: Lose the egos, win the titles.

I press on toward the goal for the prize (Philippians 3:14).

In Paul's Letter to the Philippians, he alludes to every running back's objective: reaching the goal line, pay dirt, six points, touchdown. Since he joined the Raiders in 1999, Zack Crockett has made a career out of pressing toward the goal a yard or two at a time. As a short-yardage specialist, he is often called to keep a drive alive or score by a short burst into, or high dive over, the line. How else would a back be a valuable weapon on a team when averaging only 2.0 and 2.5 yards per carry as Crockett did for two seasons? While wearing the silver and black, Crockett gained a first down or scored a touchdown nearly half the times he touched the ball (44 percent). Not many players can make that claim.

However, Paul had something more in mind than moving down the football field when he addressed his letter to the Philippians. He spoke of a realization of not being fully formed as a spiritual being, a child of God. And of the need to stay the course, to pursue God's grace and reward with deliberate speed, to press on toward this so precious goal, this heavenly prize.

> *Not that I have already obtained this or have already reached the goal; but I press on to make it my own, because Christ Jesus has made me his own. Beloved, I do not consider that I have made it my own; but this one thing I do: forgetting what lies behind and straining forward to what lies ahead, I press on toward the goal for the prize of the heavenly call of God in Christ Jesus (3:12–14).*

We can all learn a lesson from the teamwork and dedication demonstrated in football. If more of the world were not to be so concerned with selfish pursuits and instead concentrated on working together toward a common goal, imagine what we might accomplish. Perhaps Israel and Palestine could find common ground. Democrats and Republicans could work together to provide health care for every American. A husband and wife might work a little harder to overcome perceived differences.

On the gridiron, teams work as one to achieve their full reward, a Super Bowl championship. In the Bible, both Paul and John urge us all to work together to adhere to the Word of God, so that we too might receive our full reward—life everlasting with our Father who art in heaven.

THE DRAFT: PLAYERS AND APOSTLES

THE GAME OF FOOTBALL, we noted earlier, evolved from the English games of football (soccer) and rugby. Initially, teams were formed on the college level or by local athletic clubs. Leagues came and went and seasons could be all of two games long. Once players found they could earn money for playing the game, they jumped from one team to another, enticed by better salaries. Teams tried to gain an upper hand by using players who were still in college.

In trying to bring order to the game, teams met in 1920 and agreed upon a set of rules for the game and regulations for franchise operations, thus forming the American Professional Football Association, later to become the National Football League. In what was thought to be the first official transaction of the APFA, tackle Bob Nash was sold from the Akron Pros to the Buffalo All-Americans for the grand sum of $300—and 5 percent of the gate receipts from the Akron-Buffalo game.[1] Keep in mind that tickets may have cost in the neighborhood of 25 cents in those days, as opposed to the $100 or more for some games today. Another early development was the granting of "territories" to teams from which they could sign players. This was done in part to help keep popular local players playing for nearby pro teams in the hopes of boosting attendance and developing fan loyalty.

In 1935, as a way to help achieve a better balance of power among its teams, the NFL instituted its annual draft of college players, with teams selecting in inverse order of how they finished the previous season. In other words, the poorest performing teams had the most opportunity to choose the best college players.

A year later the first draft was held with Heisman Trophy winner Jay Berwanger of the University of Chicago becoming the first player ever so selected. After drafting Berwanger, the Philadelphia Eagles traded him to the Chicago Bears. Unfortunately, the number one choice never played as a professional, so the distinction of the first player to be drafted and actually play fell to the number two pick of the 1936 draft, Riley Smith of Alabama.[2]

These days the NFL draft is a huge operation. Scores of scouts, front-office people, and coaches view days of videotape, watch thousands of players perform in hundreds of games. College players are called in for interviews to gauge their personality, temperament, intelligence, and feel for the game. Combines are held where multiple teams gather to evaluate a number of players at once. Players are timed in the 40-yard dash and asked to repeatedly bench press 225 pounds until exhausted. NFL personnel run the college hopefuls through agility drills, test leaping ability, and administer aptitude tests. Given that a number one draft choice can make or break a team, not to mention sign a giant-sized contract, teams want to be as certain as they possibly can that they are selecting the best player to fit their needs.

Every draft holds its fair share of surprises and intrigue. In 2006, for instance, the prospective number one pick seemed to be handicapped like a horserace among USC Heisman Trophy-winning (2005) running back Reggie Bush, USC Heisman Trophy-winning (2004) quarterback Matt Leinart, and national champion Texas quarterback Vince Young. Houston held the number one pick and the Texans were thought to be enamored with home state product Young. Others thought they'd go for the explosive Bush. As draft day approached, the Texans did neither, opting to draft North Carolina State defensive end Mario Williams, rationalizing that he would be less expensive to sign than Bush, while providing their defense with an impact player. At number two, New Orleans jumped at the chance to choose Southern California's Bush. Given that Louisiana was still suffering the devastation of Hurricane Katrina, the tailback's selection was a godsend for Saints fans. But then in Exodus, God did appear to Moses as a burning bush. QB Young was nabbed by the Tennessee Titans with the third pick, while fellow quarterback Leinart, thought by many to be the best college football player in the 2005 season as well as a possible number one selection in 2006, fell all the way to the tenth spot, where he was gratefully grabbed by the Arizona Cardinals.

Franchises select players to round out their teams, either choosing to fill a particular need or grabbing the best player available when their turn comes. In this way, and augmented by free agent signings, over the years teams build the core of players that they feel best have the skills and mentality to take them to the next level, the playoffs, and ultimately a Super Bowl championship.

As I discussed in *And God Said, "Play Ball!"* Jesus also "drafted" his own team, the Galilean Apostles of the old River Jordan League. Just as newspapers, ESPN, and FOX Sports cover the NFL draft, the gospel writers did the same some two thousand years ago. Let's pick up Luke's Gospel involving Jesus, Peter, and The Catch, already in progress:

When he had finished speaking, he said to Simon, "Put out into the deep water and let down your nets for a catch." Simon answered, "Master, we have worked all night long but have caught nothing. Yet if you say so, I will let down the nets." When they had done this, they caught so many fish that their nets were beginning to break. So they signaled their partners in the other boat to come and help them. And they came and filled both boats, so that they began to sink. But when Simon Peter saw it, he fell down at Jesus' knees, saying "Go away from me, Lord, for I am a sinful man!" For he and all who were with him were amazed at the catch of fish that they had taken; and so also were James and John, sons of Zebedee, who were partners with Simon. Then Jesus said to Simon, "Do not be afraid; from now on you will be catching people." When they had brought their boats to shore, they left everything and followed him (5:4–11).

While NFL general managers and head coaches seek the most talented athletes to fill their rosters, Jesus took a slightly different approach. Instead of choosing political or religious leaders of his day, the rich or influential, Christ personally selected simple fishermen and common people. He even handpicked a member of society from whom the Jews traditionally distanced themselves—a tax collector. Given that Palestine was under Roman domination, inhabitants had to pay Caesar what was Caesar's, and then some. Tax collectors were typically Jews in the employ of the Roman government. Any sum over and above what was due Rome usually lined their pockets. As you might imagine, such "civil" servants were not welcome with open arms as their wealth came at the people's expense. Yet, Jesus specifically called on one such individual to join his team.

As Jesus was walking along, he saw a man named Matthew sitting at the tax booth; and he said to him, "Follow me." And he got up and followed him.

And as he sat at dinner in the house, many tax collectors and sinners came and were sitting with him and his disciples. When the Pharisees saw this, they said to his disciples, "Why does your teacher eat with tax collectors and sinners?" But when he heard this, he said, "Those who are well have no need of a physician, but those who are sick. Go and learn what this means, 'I desire mercy, not sacrifice.' For I have come to call not the righteous but sinners" (Matthew 9:9–13).

From John's Gospel comes the drafting of more "players":

The next day Jesus decided to go to Galilee. He found Philip

and said to him, "Follow me." Now Philip was from Beth-
saida, the city of Andrew and Peter. Philip found Nathanael
and said to him, "We have found him about whom Moses
in the law and also the prophets wrote, Jesus son of Joseph
from Nazareth." Nathanael said to him, "Can anything
good come out of Nazareth?" Philip said to him, "Come
and see." When Jesus saw Nathanael coming toward him,
he said…"I saw you under the fig tree before Philip called
you." Nathanael replied, "Rabbi, you are the Son of God!
You are the King of Israel!" (1:43–49).

Finally, Mark sums up the rest of Christ's selections in this way:

He went up to the mountain and called to him those whom
he wanted, and they came to him. And he appointed twelve,
whom he also named apostles, to be with him, and to be
sent out to proclaim the message, and to have authority to
cast out demons. So he appointed the twelve: Simon (to
whom he gave the name Peter); James son of Zebedee and
John the brother of James (to whom he gave the name Bo-
anerges, that is, Sons of Thunder); and Andrew, and Philip,
and Bartholomew [Nathanael], and Matthew, and Thomas,
and James son of Alphaeus, and Thaddaeus, and Simon the
Cananaean, and Judas Iscariot… (3:13–19).

Analyzing Jesus' draft, we realize that there is great hope for the
larger team of humanity. Think about whom Christ chose. Peter
admitted he was a sinful man. Matthew was scorned as a pawn of
the Roman government. Nathanael was initially skeptical about
Jesus and his ministry: "Can anything good come out of Nazareth?"
Later in the gospels, we learn that Thomas was a cynic, thus the
term *doubting Thomas.*

Jesus did not choose the righteous, the powerful, the influential, the rich. He chose the everyman…the sinner, skeptic, cynic,

scorned. In other words, Christ has chosen us. Through his teachings, preaching, passion, death, and resurrection, the Son of God has redeemed us all.

NFL minds wonder if anything good can come from a seventeenth-round draft pick. Then Bart Starr shines bright for the Green Bay Packers. Football people question if anything can come from the 199th person chosen in the draft. Sixth-round selection Tom Brady leads the Patriots to three titles in four years. Can anything good come out of Nazareth? Jesus Christ conquers death and sin, giving hope to humanity. An aristocrat named Ignatius comes out of Spain to form the Jesuit Order. Agnes Gonxha Bojaxhiu is born in Skopje, Macedonia, and earns the Nobel Peace Prize as Mother Teresa. A goalie in his youth and later a volunteer librarian, Karol Josef Wojtyla never forgot his Polish roots even after becoming the beloved Pope John Paul II. So, too, are we capable of great things, whether they be the raising of our children, helping out at a hospital, joining Habitat for Humanity to help rebuild New Orleans, or offering a smile to a complete stranger.

Can anything good come out of Nazareth? Darn straight it can!

Of course, there are those draft picks that don't work out, no matter how many films are watched, how many statistics analyzed, or how many times a player is interviewed.

For instance, Anthony Davis, a former USC tailback, is in the college football Hall of Fame. Drafted by the Tampa Bay Buccaneers in 1974, after a season with the World Football League, he opted to play for the Toronto Argonauts of the Canadian Football League. When he finally joined the Bucs in 1977 he scored a single touchdown for the team. This from a college player who scored six touchdowns against Notre Dame—in a single game. Playing for two teams the next year, Davis rushed for all of seven yards on three carries. Offensive lineman Tony Mandarich was drafted number two overall in 1989. Rather than live up to his hype, he lived up to his position. In short, he was offensive. For the longest time he was considered one of the biggest busts in draft history, especially when

Green Bay could have chosen either Barry Sanders or Deion Sanders in the same draft. The Packers cut him three years into a four-year contract. Similarly, in 1991 the Seattle Seahawks passed on quarterback Brett Favre in favor of San Diego State's Dan McGwire. At six foot eight inches tall, McGwire was long on height. It's just that he was short on NFL skills. In four years with the team he threw a grand total of two touchdown passes.

Without a doubt, the most-wasted draft choice of recent memory occurred in the 1998 draft. Quarterbacks Peyton Manning from Tennessee and Washington State's Ryan Leaf were considered to be the top two players in the draft in virtually every report. Holding the top three spots in the draft were the Colts, Cardinals, and Chargers. Hoping to ensure that they'd get one player or the other, San Diego made a big trade with Arizona to move up to the second slot. Selecting first, Indianapolis had to decide between the former Volunteer and Cougar. As the football world knows, the Colts took Manning and developed into a playoff contender. That left Leaf to the Chargers, who quickly bestowed a four-year contract on the QB worth $31.25 million, including an $11.25 million signing bonus.[3]

Fast-forward four years later. Leaf's numbers for the Chargers were less than dazzling: 14 touchdowns, 36 interceptions, 48.4 percent of his passes completed. Yes, that's less than half. Meanwhile during the same period, Manning threw for 111 scores against 81 picks, completing 61 percent of his passes. While Manning showed leadership, Leaf demonstrated immaturity. His teammates and management quickly soured on his behavior. Had he been able to produce on the field, perhaps the locker room outbursts would have been overlooked. However, results count in the NFL. Thus, Ryan Leaf threw his last pass during the 2001 season. Whereas Peyton Manning continued to only get better. His accomplishments include a Most Valuable Player award and the NFL record for most touchdown passes thrown in a single season with 49, and a victory in Super Bowl XLI.

Pro football general managers aren't the only ones to occasionally make a regrettable choice. Of Jesus' twelve apostles, one died in infamy. Judas Iscariot will forever be known as the man who handed Jesus over to the authorities, precipitating Christ's arrest, trial, scourging. and crucifixion. Mark first describes the man as, *Judas Iscariot, who betrayed him* (3:19). Christ himself said, *"...woe to that one by whom the Son of Man is betrayed! It would have been better for that one not to have been born"* (Matthew 26:24).

There are times in our lives when we have made poor choices or, when chosen, do not live up to expectations, whether our own or those placed upon us by others. For his part, Judas was disconsolate over his actions, so much so that he hanged himself. Jesus does not want us to be so inconsolable that we turn our back on the Father. Our thoughts, words, or actions may betray God, but he never abandons us. Whatever our transgression, we are given an opportunity for redemption—a redemption that Christ won for us by his death on the cross.

Things are rarely so bad that they cannot be made better. Consider the Chargers. Despite drafting Ryan Leaf, they have prospered. Under the guidance of quarterback Stan Humphries, the Chargers advanced to Super Bowl XXIX. With Drew Brees at the helm, the 'bolts returned to the playoffs in 2004.

Having one of their team betray Christ could have caused the apostles to lose faith and question everything. Yet Christ overcame death. Matthias replaced Judas as a member of the twelve. And Jesus' team spread the Good News that is his death and resurrection.

"For nothing will be impossible with God" (Luke 1:37).

PLAYERS AND PARABLES

DURING HIS PUBLIC MINISTRY, that is, the last few years of his life spent preaching and teaching, Christ introduced a number of social and spiritual themes, among them forgiveness, service, sacrifice, inclusion, equality. Many were quite revolutionary for the time and still a challenge for many well-meaning people today.

In Peter's third denial of Christ, the apostle exclaimed, "I do not know the man!" In a sense it could be said that Peter really didn't know the man. Jesus was someone who government authorities viewed as a rebel, and religious leaders saw as sacrilegious and a threat to their power. Neighbors mocked him and even his closest associates did not understand his teachings. Here was a man who could heal the sick, give sight to the blind, drive demons out, walk on water, and raise the dead. He also predicted his own death and resurrection three days later! How in the world are we to understand such a one as this?

That's where parables come in.

Jesus often used parables to teach and reach his followers—similar to an Aesop's fable with a spiritual lesson attached to teach and reach his followers. This was in part because his message was so contrary to the teachings of that time, he had to couch them in terms that were more palatable to the masses and religious leaders alike. And what could be more acceptable than what was in effect a children's bedtime story for an older audience. Parables are scattered throughout all the gospels, all told with a life lesson in mind...and in some cases with a reference to football as well.

To set the stage, however, I'd like to just touch upon some odds and (tight) ends connecting matters of faith and football. For instance, from Exodus comes one of the first references to uniforms.

[B]lue, purple, and crimson (Exodus 25:4).

In developing his covenant with the Jews, God sought gifts from them, freely given, including gold, silver, and bronze; and blue, purple, and crimson thread. This set the tone for our relationship with our Father. He will love us and be true to us forever. All he asks in return is that we give voluntarily of our time, treasure, or talent. Just as he has bestowed these gifts on us, we are asked to bestow our gifts on others.

Not only did we receive these instructions but also a variety of vibrant colors for football uniforms. Perhaps unknowingly the NFL has taken God's words to heart and offers him a dazzling array of brightly colored football uniforms in thanks for the gridiron gifts he has bestowed.

Take a look around the league. Wearing some sort of blue are the Bears, Broncos, Chargers, Colts, and Panthers. Donning a shade of red are the Buccaneers, Cardinals, Chiefs, and Redskins. Combining red and blue are the Bills, Giants, Patriots, Texans, and Titans, while the 49ers wear red and gold, and the Rams blue and gold. Some form of blue and silver are the colors of the Cowboys, Lions, and Seahawks. Silver is one of the Raiders' colors, and gold is one of the Saints'. Lastly, adorned in purple are the Ravens and Vikings. Whew!

Colors also play a part in the vestments worn by priests as they celebrate the Catholic Mass. Generally speaking, here's how the raiment rainbow is divided. Symbolizing growth, green is worn during Ordinary Time, which includes most Mass days of the year. White, as in other cultures, is the symbol of purity or light. Used in celebrations of rejoicing, it is worn on special feasts such as Corpus Christi, during festive occasions such as baptisms and weddings, and on Christmas and Easter. Black or white vestments may be worn during funerals, black to suggest mourning, white to suggest resurrection. Some parishes use white vestments trimmed in blue for feasts of Mary. Gold vestments, or white with gold, may be used for very special occasions such as Christmas and Easter. Red, the color of blood, is worn to celebrate the feasts of martyrs, as well as on Pentecost Sunday, when the Holy Spirit descended upon the apostles as if by tongues of fire. Red is also used on Good Friday to commemorate Christ's crucifixion and death, while a shade of red, rose, is used during the Third Sunday of Advent and the Fourth Sunday of Lent. As a sign of penance and dignity, purple is worn during the preparatory seasons of Advent and Lent.

Moving from team colors to team names, three franchises have direct ties with things Catholic. While the Arizona Cardinals seem to be named after the red bird with the crested crown, football-friendly clergy members no doubt muse upon the college of Cardinals, that order of specially ordained bishops who have the responsibility for electing the pope. The New Orleans Saints call to mind the communion of saints, that ever-expanding body of souls who have attained heaven. While the football Saints go marching in on Sunday afternoons, Catholics and Christians march to service on Sunday in the hopes of eventually calling the kingdom of heaven their home. Lastly, St. Louis is the city and football team named after Louis IX, King of France and saint of the Catholic Church. Crowned as king at age twelve, Louis became known for his works of charity, having built hospitals, libraries, orphanages, cathedrals, and churches during his reign. He was canonized in 1297.

Now to paraphrase the opening to *Monday Night Football*: Are you ready for some parables!?!

When he was alone, those who were around him along with the twelve asked him about the parables. And he said to them, "To you has been given the secret of the kingdom of God, but for those outside, everything comes in parables" (Mark 4:10–11).

"The reason I speak to them in parables is that 'seeing they do not perceive, and hearing they do not listen, nor do they understand.' With them indeed is fulfilled the prophecy of Isaiah that says:
'You will indeed listen, but never understand,
    and you will indeed look, but never perceive.
For this people's heart has grown dull,
    and their ears are hard of hearing,
    and they have shut their eyes;
    so that they might not look with their eyes,
and listen with their ears,
and understand with their heart and turn—
    and I would heal them' " (Matthew 13:14–15).

So that we might see and perceive, hear and understand, let us visit a pair of parables, a teaching or two, and see what we might learn of the kingdom of God and the game of the gridiron.

"The kingdom of heaven is like treasure hidden in a field, which someone found and hid; then in his joy he goes and sells all that he has and buys that field.
    "Again, the kingdom of heaven is like a merchant in search of fine pearls; on finding one pearl of great value, he went and sold all that he had and bought it" (Matthew 13:44–46).

In these two parables, the kingdom of heaven is likened to an item of great value. Whether we come across our faith by accident as in the case of the man who stumbled across treasure hidden in a field, or through diligent searching as with the merchant and the pearl, the joy of heaven is beyond our wildest dreams, so much so that we should do everything in our power to make ourselves worthy of entrance to the kingdom.

To the practical among us, these parables may not make much sense. Should we sell all that we have to own a treasure in a field or a pearl of great price, we would be exchanging our home, car, and belongings for a prized possession. In order to have shelter, food, or transportation, we would have to sell a portion of our treasure or sell the pearl. Who would be so enamored of something to give up all of what they own to have it? Ah, one need only turn to football for an example or three.

Before Gale Sayers was the next coming of Bobby Mitchell, Bobby Mitchell was the next coming of Ollie Matson. As a Chicago Cardinal and Los Angeles Ram, Matson showed a flair for scoring that few have matched before or since. His particular combination of speed and elusiveness proved lethal from nearly anywhere on the field, as attested to by his 40 rushing touchdowns, 23 receiving scores, 6 kickoff returns, 3 punt take backs, and a fumble recovery returned for a score. As such a valuable and versatile a player, Matson was obtained in 1959 by the Rams in a trade with the Cards—for nine players. That is not a misprint. Nine players, including two tackles, one each of a defensive end, end, halfback and fullback, plus a second-round draft pick and a player to be named later.[1]

A trade anomaly? A once in a league transaction? Hardly. During the 1999 draft, then New Orleans coach Mike Ditka traded every draft selection the Saints had, plus the first and third in 2000 to Washington for the rights to draft and sign University of Texas running back Ricky Williams. To Ditka, Williams was such a valuable commodity he was willing to "sell everything he owned" in order to draft him.

As amazing as those two trades were, they're a good third-and-long from the biggest transaction in NFL history. Like the Matson and Williams deals, this one centered on a premier running back, Herschel Walker. Despite playing his first few seasons in the now defunct United States Football League, Walker averaged more than

1,500 all-purpose yards for twelve NFL seasons, scoring 82 TDs along the way, 61 on the ground, 21 by air. He was such a rushing, receiving, and return threat that the Minnesota Vikings sought him in a trade with the Dallas Cowboys. By the time the ink had dried on the 1989 deal, eighteen bodies had been exchanged! Not only that but it took nearly an entire football season to sort the trade out. Not really, but it certainly seemed that way.

Minnesota received Walker and three draft choices over two years from Dallas. In return, the Vikings sent the Cowboys linebackers Jesse Solomon and David Howard, cornerback Isaac Holt, and defensive end Alex Stewart, along with eight draft choices over three years. Minnesota also traded running back Darrin Nelson to Dallas, who in turn shipped him to the Chargers for a draft pick that the Cowboys sent back to the Vikes.[2] Now that's a trade!

Unfortunately, in each case, none of the three trades worked out for the teams acquiring the marquee players. Only twice during Matson's career did he play on a team that finished above .500. Mike Ditka was fired by the Saints for the team's poor performance, and after three seasons Ricky Williams was traded to the Dolphins, despite two 1,000-yard years. Walker, too, spent only three years with his new team before moving on to the Philadelphia Eagles. At least Herschel helped the Vikings make the playoffs his first year, though they promptly lost in the opening round.

Perhaps there's a lesson to be learned here as well. All too often, we seek to obtain happiness through consumption, addiction, or even transactions. A new car or plasma TV may provide initial thrills, but ultimately they will fail us in times of emotional need. Drugs or alcohol may help make the pain of divorce and other perceived human failures go away. Temporarily. Then the vicious cycle repeats itself. General managers may trade any number of players for a star, or spend tremendous amounts of money to sign a draft pick or free agent, only to be disappointed by that player's performance or have his career unfortunately cut short by injury. As Jesus has taught us, the only way to eternal happiness, to heaven, is through the Father.

If only we could exchange a little of the time we devote to earthly pleasures for more time spent pursuing what God holds in store for us. Now that would be a great trade.

Not only can we learn lessons from parables but also from the two-minute warning. Before the end of each half of a football game, the clock stops at the two-minute mark. This is to let both teams know that time is winding down. Should the team on offense be behind, they will go into their two-minute drill, a special series of plays that allow them to gain the most number of yards in the least amount of time.

Life on occasion will give us a two-minute warning. Someone heretofore healthy suffers a surprise heart attack. A driver narrowly avoids a potentially fatal accident. Cancer is detected early enough to be successfully treated. Events like these oftentimes come with a spiritual component attached. We realize that time is short, life is precious. We see the world differently. Colors are brighter, smells more fragrant, old slights seem less important now, relationships, especially with our Maker, become paramount in our lives. However, many of us never receive the equivalent of a two-minute warning. Or if we do, we come to eventually ignore it. For us, there is another parable in Jesus' own words.

> *"But in those days, after that suffering,*
> *the sun will be darkened,*
> *and the moon will not give off its light,*
> *and the stars will be falling from heaven,*
> *and the powers in the heavens will be shaken.*
> *Then they will see 'the Son of Man coming in the clouds'*
> *with great power and glory. Then he will send out the angels,*
> *and gather his elect from the four winds, from the ends of*
> *the earth to the ends of heaven....*
>
> *"But about that day or hour no one knows, neither the*
> *angels in heaven, nor the Son, but only the Father. Beware,*
> *keep alert; for you do not know when the time will come.*

It is like a man going on a journey, when he leaves home and puts his slaves in charge, each with his work, and commands the doorkeeper to be on the watch. Therefore, keep awake—for you do not know when the master of the house will come, in the evening, or at midnight, or at cockcrow, or at dawn, or else he may find you asleep when he comes suddenly. And what I say to you I say to all: Keep awake" (Mark 13:24–28, 32–37).

In these words, Jesus has given each of us our own personal two-minute warning. As sure as John Elway could orchestrate a come-from-behind win, our time will come when we are called home to God. Will we be worthy of the room our Father has prepared for us? That all depends on how well we've lived our lives, the sorrow in our hearts for our own failings, and the forgiveness we have of others. Every day is an opportunity for us to go into our "two-minute drill" to ensure that we are in a right relationship with the world and our Father:

"Keep awake therefore, for you do not know on what day your Lord is coming. But understand this: if the owner of the house had known in what part of the night the thief was coming, he would have stayed awake and would not have let his house be broken into. Therefore you also must be ready, for the Son of Man is coming at an unexpected hour" (Matthew 24:42–44).

For a lesson as to how to live our lives, we turn to the gospel of an ex-tax collector and the example of a former Detroit Lion.

Then someone came to him and said, "Teacher, what good deed must I do to have eternal life?" And he said to him, "Why do you ask me about what is good? There is only one who is good. If you wish to enter into life, keep the commandments." He said to him, "Which ones?" And Jesus said, "You

*shall not murder; You shall not commit adultery; You shall
not steal; You shall not bear false witness; Honor your father
and mother; also, You shall love your neighbor as yourself."
The young man said to him, "I have kept all these; what do
I still lack?" Jesus said to him, "If you wish to be perfect, go,
sell your possessions, and give the money to the poor, and you
will have treasure in heaven; then come, follow me." When
the young man heard this word, he went away grieving, for
he had many possessions* (Matthew 19:16–22).

In this set of instructions from Jesus, we learn it is not enough to
just obey the commandments. We are called to do more than just
faithfully attend Mass and receive the sacraments. We must also
serve by contributing of our time, treasure, and talent to those in
need. All too often, we find that our possessions actually possess us.
It may be a desire to own the latest in fashion season after season,
to own the biggest TV or the fastest car. We may fall into being possessed by our kids' busy schedules, driving them to piano, soccer,
lacrosse, baseball, swimming, ballet, the tutor, to parties. None of
these things is bad in and of themselves. But when we find ourselves
paying more attention to a plasma TV rather than poverty, to a
fancy SUV instead of homelessness, filling time with activities rather
than spending time as a family, then our focus is misplaced. God
has bestowed on us gifts not so that we can accumulate as much as
possible, but so that we can share as much as we can.

*"From everyone to whom much has been given, much will
be required; and from the one to whom much has been
entrusted, even more will be demanded"* (Luke 12:48).

For the rich man in the above story, he was faced with a life-changing
decision. He was a man of great possessions; he had accumulated
much. No doubt he appreciated his wealth and lavish lifestyle. In
his case, to gain the kingdom he would have to give up his earthly

riches. In part, Detroit running back Barry Sanders had a similar decision.

At the age of thirty-one, having accumulated 15,269 yards rushing, Sanders was a typical Barry season away from breaking Walter Payton's record for most yards gained rushing in a career. What's more, still in good health, Sanders could have added to his total for years to come. With an NFL record within his grasp plus the attendant accolades, not to mention several million dollars in salary, Sanders walked away. To him, the record was not as important as his personal reasons for retiring. More yards and more money were not the issues. More peace of mind was. In this particular instance, Barry Sanders let go of the demands the record, his team, and NFL fans placed on him. Given the choice of following his heart or being possessed by the fame and the game, Sanders in effect gave away the record that was his for the taking.

For many Americans and others, we spend most of our lives working hard to live better, to provide for our children and grandchildren, to capture the American dream. Being asked to do otherwise seems contrary to our way of life. Even the disciples thought so.

> Then Jesus said to his disciples, "Truly I tell you, it will be hard for a rich person to enter the kingdom of heaven. Again I tell you, it is easier for a camel to go through the eye of a needle than for someone who is rich to enter the kingdom of God." When the disciples heard this, they were greatly astounded and said, "Then who can be saved?" But Jesus looked at them and said, "For mortals it is impossible, but for God all things are possible" (Matthew 19:23–26).

We have been made in God's image and likeness. Christ teaches us to love our neighbors as ourselves. In other words, we are to see God in all of those around us, friends and neighbors, enemies and strangers. In so doing, it becomes much easier to give of ourselves. God within us is touched by God in another. An earthquake rocks Pakistan; we open up our hearts to its victims. Hurricane Katrina devastates the Gulf Coast; we give what we have to those who have not.

These are huge first steps for us all. We feel compassion for our fellow men and women affected by AIDs in Africa; we mourn for those thousands murdered in the tribal wars of the Sudan. Our compassion turns to passion; our passion turns to action. We donate our time, talent, our treasure. What God gives to us, we give to others.

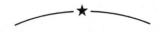

TALENTS AND TOUCHDOWNS

OF THE FIFTY-THREE MEMBERS who make up the modern pro football team roster, there are men of all shapes and sizes, speed and skills. Compare someone the size of a house to a kick return specialist. Former tackle Howard "House" Ballard measured six feet six inches tall and 325 pounds wide, while Dante Hall checks in at all of five feet eight inches tall and 187 pounds.

As for skills, offensive linemen must open holes for running backs and provide pass protection for quarterbacks. Both duties require fending off hard-charging defensive behemoths. Quarterbacks have the ability to read the defense and quickly react, throwing fifty-yard bombs, fifteen-yard fades, and bullets across the middle with equal effect. Halfbacks have the speed to get around to the outside or to exploit a hole up the middle. In the open field they demonstrate the ability to change direction quickly with any number of fakes, jukes, spin moves, hurdles, and cutbacks. Fullbacks must take on defensive linemen and linebackers while blocking for halfbacks, yet be able to run with and catch the ball. Similarly, tight ends are called on to be both blockers and receivers.

On the other side of the ball, defensive linemen must be able to shed blocks and tackle ball carriers, plus rush the passer. Linebackers need to be able to stop the run and cover backs coming out of the backfield. Safeties and cornerbacks are responsible for covering fleet-footed receivers displaying elusive moves, as well as tackling runners who have burst past the first two lines of defense.

On special teams, punters must loft kicks high and far, pinning the opposition deep in their own territory. Place kickers must boot extra points and field goals with unerring accuracy, often in miserable conditions from great distances with the game on the line. Deep snappers must in effect throw a fifteen-yard pass through their legs while looking at their punter upside down at the same time knowing they're going to be crushed by a charging defensive lineman. Holders must take the snap from center, place the ball quickly down at just the right angle with the laces facing away from the oncoming place kicker. Members of the "suicide" squad must speed downfield with reckless abandon to take on blockers and upend kick and punt returners.

In the stands, there are just as many different types of people with their own areas of expertise. We may not know it by looking at them, what with their faces painted silver and black or green and blue, or wearing dog masks or waving terrible towels, but numbered among football fans are physicians who heal, parents who nurture, teachers who educate, carpenters who build, mechanics who repair, architects who design, performers who entertain, merchants who provide, farmers who grow, police and fire personnel who protect.

In short, God has given each and every one of us our own gifts, our own talents. He expects us to nurture them and share them to the best of our abilities.

> *"For it is as if a man, going on a journey, summoned his slaves and entrusted his property to them; to one he gave five talents, to another two, to another one, to each according to his ability. Then he went away. The one who had received the five talents went off at once and traded with them, and made five more talents. In the same way, the one who had the two talents made two more talents. But the one who received one talent went off and dug a hole in the ground*

and hid his master's money. After a long time the master of
those slaves came and settled accounts with them. Then the
one who had received five talents came forward, bringing
five more talents, saying, 'Master, you handed over to me
five talents; see, I have made five more talents.' His master
said to him, 'Well done, good and trustworthy slave; you
have been trustworthy in a few things, I will put you in
charge of many things; enter into the joy of your master.'
And the one with the two talents also came forward, saying, 'Master, you handed over to me two talents; see, I have
made two more talents.' His master said to him, 'Well done,
good and trustworthy slave; you have been trustworthy
in a few things, I will put you in charge of many things;
enter into the joy of your master.' Then the one who had
received one talent also came forward, saying, 'Master, I
knew that you were a harsh man, reaping where you did
not sow, and gathering where you did not scatter seed; so
I was afraid, and I went and hid your talent in the ground.
Here you have what is yours.' But his master replied, 'You
wicked and lazy slave! You knew, did you, that I reap where
I do not sow, and gather where I did not scatter? Then you
ought to have invested my money with the bankers, and on
my return I would have received what was my own with
interest. So take the talent from him, and give it to the one
with the ten talents. For to all those who have, more will
be given, and they will have an abundance; but from those
who have nothing, even what they have will be taken away.
As for this worthless slave, throw him into the outer darkness, where there will be weeping and gnashing of teeth'"
(Matthew 25:14–30).

In football and in life, there have been individuals who have been
given unique gifts who have allowed them to flourish. And there have
been those who have been given talents and squandered them.

In the 1960s, All-Pro Paul Hornung of the Green Bay Packers and Alex Karras of the Detroit Loins were suspended for a year for gambling. Ryan Leaf could throw the football like few college quarterbacks, yet his immaturity cost him his career. Thomas "Hollywood" Henderson derailed an All-Pro career as a linebacker with the Dallas Cowboys by his addiction to crack cocaine. Similarly, first-round draft choice Todd Marinovich of the Los Angeles Raiders saw his playing days as a quarterback come to a premature end due to drugs, while Miami Dolphin running back Ricky Williams has constantly battled marijuana problems throughout his on-again, off-again career. Art Schlichter's promising tenure as a QB folded due to a gambling addiction, which led to writing bad checks, which led to jail time. Bill Romanowski had an award-winning career, but his use of performance-enhancing drugs caused him to assault a teammate. Likewise Lyle Alzado's reliance on illegal substances led to an early death due to brain cancer.

Fortunately, football provides us with many more examples of those who nurtured their talents. Several with dual talents spring immediately to mind. Roger Craig of the 49ers was the first player ever (and Marshall Faulk the only other one) to amass more than 1,000 yards rushing and receiving in a single season. 'Niner QB Steve Young had a rushing career that many running backs would envy, running for 4,239 yards and 43 scores. That he also threw for 33,124 yards and 232 touchdowns makes this all the more remarkable. Young averaged an impressive 5.9 yards a carry, and his career passing rating of 96.8 is the best all time. However, perhaps the most amazing display of two talents came via a lineman.

In the early days of the sport, players were required to play both on offense and defense for the entire game. That's how in 1943 Sammy Baugh could lead the league in passing and passes intercepted, not to mention punting. It should be noted that many quarterbacks have led the league interceptions. However, those are passes they threw that were intercepted. Baugh's interceptions came while he was playing defense.

Chuck Bednarik, however, puts an end to all talk about making the most use of two talents. A nine-time All-Pro from the Philadelphia Eagles, Bednarik played on both sides of the ball. In a career that spanned three decades from 1949 to 1962, he built a well-deserved reputation as a bone-crushing blocker and a teeth-rattling tackler. No wonder he is acknowledged as football's iron man.

As with most games, the team that scores the most points wins. So the individuals who can score the most points in the most ways are quite special. Football has been blessed with notable players who have demonstrated remarkable scoring virtuosity. These rare performers had the talents to score in five—count them—five different ways!

Balance, moves, and speed. Such was the combination possessed by Bobby Mitchell, an All-Pro running back and flanker for the Cleveland Browns and Washington Redskins. Talk about showcasing talents. Mitchell made the Pro Bowl four times. That's not so unusual; the great players are named to the team year after year. However, Mitchell was honored once as a running back and three times as a receiver. He was, indeed, a star, a five-point star with each point representing a way of scoring. At his retirement, Mitchell had accumulated more than 14,000 combined net yards, second most ever at the time. He crossed the goal line nearly every way imaginable and plenty of times: 18 rushing TDs, 65 receiving, 3 via punt returns, and 5 kickoff returns. He also was three for three as a passer in his career for 61 yards. As if to put icing on the scoring machine cake, one of those passes was thrown for a touchdown.

There will probably never be another Bobby Mitchell. That is unless his name is Gale Sayers. Sayers was as fleet as he was nimble. Any time he touched the ball, he was a threat to score. As if to prove the point, in his rookie season with Chicago he totaled six touchdowns—in a single game. That it came against my 49ers was nearly too much to take. Included in the scoring barrage was an 80-yard pass, catch, and run; a 50-yard rushing TD; and a 65-yard punt return.[1] I remember listening to the game on the radio thinking to myself, *Can't anyone tackle this guy?* I imagine over the course of his career, many others asked the same question. His playing days were cut short by injury. He amassed the Lions', or should I say Bears', share, of his stats in just five seasons. His career scoring repertoire included 39 rushing TDs, 9 by pass, 6 kickoff returns, 2 punt returns, and a partridge in a pear tree. Make that a pass thrown for a touchdown.

Not one to let the offensive players have all the fun, and certainly not shy of the spotlight, defensive back Deion Sanders calls to mind a verse from the Book of Ruth:

...and may his name be [famous]..." (4:14).

In Scripture the passage referred to Ruth's son by Boaz, who was to be called Obed, who became the father of Jesse, who became the father of David, from whose line did Jesus come. In sport, the verse refers to Sanders, whose own name was not enough to summarize the excitement he brought to the game. Thus the moniker: "Neon Deion." His exploits were such that sportswriters, and Sanders himself, needed yet another superlative to bestow on him. For his ability to play big in big games, he became known as "Primetime." Neon Deion Primetime Sanders earned every adjective that described his play. Bold and flashy, not to mention supremely talented, Sanders showcased his scoring talents this way: 9 interceptions returned for touchdowns, likewise for 3 kickoff returns, and 6 punt returns, 3 TD receptions as a wide receiver no less, and a fumble recovery returned for a score. In the constellation that makes up the NFL skies, the stars of Sanders, Sayers, and Mitchell shine among the brightest.

As the story of the talents and touchdowns has shown, we are all given certain gifts from our Creator. We may not be able to throw a football with any accuracy nor get anywhere near sacking a quarterback. But some of us have the ability to speak foreign languages or play the flute. Others are able to write software code or discover cures for diseases. Still others can walk on I-beams or mine for coal.

Regardless of the nature or the quantity of our gifts, we all have the capacity to love—the game of football and one another.

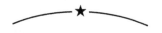

FUM-BLE!

BEING HUMAN, WE TEND TO ERR. Being gridiron gamers, we tend to err in front of 80,000 screaming fans and millions of viewers watching on television. Thanks to slow-motion instant replay, we are witness to the same mistakes over and over again for all to see. It's a fact of life. We stumble. We fumble. There's no better example of this than football—unless it's the Bible.

Fumbles, interceptions, missed tackles, and dropped passes have become part of the game. Statisticians calculate fumbles made, fumbles recovered, interceptions, interceptions returned for touchdowns, turnover ratios, points off turnovers, everything but apple turnovers. An examination of some of the more famous, or infamous, miscues even bring a sense of the sacred to the discussion with terms like Holy Roller, Immaculate Deception, and Miracle in the Meadowlands.

One of the earliest fumbles ever recorded was in 1892, when our friend William "Pudge" Heffelfinger picked up a fumble and ran 35 yards for a touchdown, giving his Allegheny Athletic Association a 4–0 victory over the Pittsburgh Athletic Club back in the day when a TD was worth four points.[1]

The year 1978 proved a year of remarkable fumbles. In the beginning of the season the Oakland Raiders were the beneficiary of some last-minute (well, last ten seconds to be accurate) shenanigans involving the bouncing ball. Down 20–14 to the San Diego Chargers, Raiders quarterback Ken "The Snake" Stabler intentionally fumbled the football forward just as he was being sacked at the San Diego

15-yard line. With time running out, Raiders running back Pete Banaszak and tight end Dave Casper ostensibly tried to recover the ball, only to push it closer to the goal line. With the ball finally lying in the end zone, Casper pounced on it for a game-tying touchdown. With a successful extra point, the Raiders won. Since the players did not seem to intentionally move the ball forward, the officials let the score stand. The controversial call led to a rule change the following season where, in the last two minutes of a game, a fumbled ball by the offense can only be recovered and advanced by the player who fumbled it in the first place.

I remember watching the game on TV. Being a Raider fan, I screamed in despair when Stabler dropped the ball only to shout for joy when Casper was awarded six points. I'm sure Charger fans reacted in a completely opposite fashion. In fact, while the play has become known as "The Holy Roller" in football circles, San Diego faithful refer to it as the Immaculate Deception.[2]

Speaking of spiritual references to football follies, no discussion of fumbles can be complete without mention of "The Miracle at the Meadowlands," a play I've seen replayed numerous times. Later during the same season that gave us The Holy Roller, the Giants and Eagles played a game at the Meadowlands in New Jersey, the Giants' home field. Leading 17–12 with half a minute to play, New York only needed to run out the clock to secure the victory. Instead of taking the snap from center and kneeling down, Giants quarterback Joe Pisarcik handed the ball off to fullback Larry Csonka for a last run into the line. Only Zonk never got his hands safely around the ball. With Pisarcik letting go and Csonka not hanging on, the ball bounced loose, only to be snatched up by Eagles cornerback Herman Edwards (now the coach of the Kansas City Chiefs), who returned it for a touchdown and a Philadelphia victory, propelling the Eagles to the playoffs.[3]

Mention The Fumble in the Cleveland area and most everyone will recall the heartache that came one cold January day in 1988. Trailing the Denver Broncos 38–31 in the AFC championship game, the Browns had driven to Denver's eight-yard line. Unfortunately, Browns running back Earnest Byner lost control of the ball to fumble away the Browns' chances to tie the game and possibly reach the Super Bowl.[4] Though a 1,000-yard rusher for the Browns, Byner was traded to the Redskins after the next season. Ironically for Cleveland fans, and thankfully for Byner, he helped the Washington Redskins claim Super Bowl XXVI. For Browns fans turned blue, the play brought back painful memories of QB Brian Sipe's pass that was intercepted seven years earlier in the final minute of Cleveland's playoff game against the Raiders, literally tossing Oakland a 14–12 victory.[5] Once again, my screams of despair turned into shouts of joy.

Dropped passes are just as much a part of the game as fumbled handoffs or interceptions. Try as wide receivers might, they can't catch everything. Of course, the most embarrassing moments for receivers come when the ball is thrown exactly to them, hits them in the numbers, and falls to the ground. Just ask Jackie Smith. After an outstanding fifteen-year career with the St. Louis Cardinals, Smith signed on with the Cowboys as a reserve tight end for the 1978 season. What should have been the capstone to a Hall of Fame career, turned out to be anything but. That year Dallas reached the Super Bowl, Smith's first. In a tightly contested battle with the Steelers, the Cowboys had an excellent opportunity to score in the second half. On third down, deep in Pittsburgh territory, quarterback Roger Staubach found Smith, alone in the middle of the Steeler end zone, and threw a sure touchdown pass—except that the reliable, sure-handed Smith dropped the ball.[6] More people judge Jackie Smith's career by that one miss rather than his 480 receptions for 7,918 yards and 40 TDs. Adding insult to ineptitude, the Cowboys had to settle for a field goal in a game they ultimately lost—by four points.

One of the most famous miscues on the gridiron occurred on a fumble recovery. In 1964, in a game against the San Francisco 49ers, Minnesota Vikings defensive lineman Jim Marshall scooped up a Billy Kilmer fumble and rumbled into the end zone for a score—except instead of returning the ball to the Vikings' end zone for a touchdown, he made his way to the 49er end of the field where he was touched for a safety.⁷ Instead of scoring six points for the Vikes, he tallied two for the 'Niners!

Football players aren't the only ones who stumble and fumble their way through life. So do kings handpicked by God in heaven and saints selected by Christ on earth.

> The LORD said to Samuel..."I will send you to Jesse the Bethlehemite, for I have provided for myself a king among his sons." ...And [Samuel] sanctified Jesse and his sons and invited them to the sacrifice.
>
> When they came, he looked on Eliab and thought, "Surely, the LORD's anointed is now before the LORD." But the LORD said to Samuel, "Do not look on his appearance or on the height of his stature, because I have rejected him; for the LORD does not see as mortals see; they look on the outward appearance, but the LORD looks on the heart...." Jesse made seven of his sons pass before Samuel, and Samuel said to Jesse, "The LORD has not chosen any of these." Samuel said to Jesse, "Are all your sons here?" And he said, "There remains yet the youngest, but he is keeping the sheep." And Samuel said to Jesse, "Send and bring him; for we will not sit down until he comes here." He sent and brought him in. Now he was ruddy, and had beautiful eyes, and was handsome. The LORD said, "Rise and anoint him; for this is the one." ...and the spirit of the LORD came mightily on David from that day forward (1 Samuel 16:1, 5–7, 10–13).

God selected young David to lead his people. And David did not disappoint, at least at first. By virtue of his defeating Goliath on the field of battle, young David inspired the armies of Israel and Judah to rout the Philistines. As king, David reigned over all Israel, capturing the holy city of Jerusalem in the process. An older David is also thought to have written most of the 150 psalms included in the Bible.

Unfortunately, David abused his power. He became fascinated by the wife of one of his captains. So he sent the soldier, Uriah, to die in battle, to hide the fact that David had impregnated the man's wife. David quickly married Bathsheba who bore him a son. David's joy was short-lived, however, as the baby boy did not even live long enough to be named. Even though David had been selected by God in heaven as being good of heart, he proved himself to be very human and prone to sin.

Listen to some of Jesus' remarks to and about his followers and you might wonder if Christ had selected lunkheads rather than apostles.

> When [Jesus] was alone, those who were around him along with the twelve asked him about the parables....
>
> And he said to them, "Do you not understand this parable? Then how will you understand all the parables?" (Mark 4:10, 13).

> "...you of little faith!" (Luke 12:28).

> Jesus said to him, "Have I been with you all this time, Philip, and you still do not know me?" (John 14:9).

Of all the figures in the gospels, there is probably no one who stumbles and fumbles as much as Peter. After Jesus had calmed the sea and walked on water, Peter was inspired to try to follow Christ's example, only to lack the faith to do so.

> Peter answered him, "Lord, if it is you, command me to come to you on the water." He said, "Come." So Peter got out of the boat, started walking on the water, and came toward Jesus. But when he noticed the strong wind, he became frightened, and beginning to sink, he cried out,

> *"Lord, save me!" Jesus immediately reached out his hand*
> *and caught him, saying to him, "You of little faith, why did*
> *you doubt?"* (Matthew 14:28–31).

Then when Peter did have faith in his conviction, it was misplaced.

> *From that time on, Jesus began to show his disciples that*
> *he must go to Jerusalem and undergo great suffering at*
> *the hands of the elders and chief priests and scribes, and*
> *be killed, and on the third day be raised. And Peter took*
> *him aside and began to rebuke him, saying, "God forbid it,*
> *Lord! This must never happen to you." But he turned and*
> *said to Peter, "Get behind me, Satan! You are a stumbling*
> *block to me; for you are setting your mind not on divine*
> *things but on human things"* (Matthew 16:21–23).

As if this isn't bad enough, Peter goes on to deny Jesus three times, just as Jesus predicted he would, despite Peter's protest.

> *Peter said to him, "Though all become deserters because of*
> *you, I will never desert you"* (Matthew 26:33).

Of course, Peter did stumble. Just as we all do. But if there's one person in the Bible to give us all hope, it is Peter: fisherman, husband, well-intentioned follower, headstrong, loyal, weak, faithful, often missing the mark. Peter is the perfect example of what it is to be imperfect.

Peter was one of the first to recognize Jesus was the Messiah. He is called "Satan" for trying to dissuade Jesus from his destiny on the cross. Peter believed in Jesus so much that he asked the Lord to allow him to walk on water. When Christ did so, Peter's own lack of faith caused him to sink. Jesus proclaimed Peter the rock upon whom he would build his church. Peter denied the Lord three times. Even as an apostle, he stumbles and fumbles time and again. Despite all this, Jesus forgives Peter, restores him, and believes in him so much he entrusts him with his flock.

In football, a fumble can lose a game. In faith, a stumble can lose a soul. However, through the game we are taught to learn from our mistakes, to pick ourselves up off the turf, remove the clumps of grass from our facemasks, and play on. Through the gospels, we learn that though we may stumble time and again, all we need do is seek forgiveness. Jesus died for our sins. By doing so, he is available to pick us up, dust us off, and set us right back on the path to the kingdom for as many times as we fail and fall. No wonder they call it the Good News.

Denver Broncos' quarterback John Elway scrambles during an AFC
Championship game in Denver. CORBIS

(Above) New York Giants' great Y. A. Tittle finds an open receiver in a game against the old St. Louis Cardinals. JACK ZEHRT

(Right) Former Oakland Raiders' coach and now football broadcaster John Madden in his coaching days. JACK ZEHRT

Pittsburgh running back Franco Harris (middle) makes a catch in one of football's most famous plays, called the Immaculate Reception, in a playoff game against the Oakland Raiders in 1972.

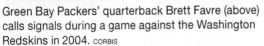

Green Bay Packers' quarterback Brett Favre (above) calls signals during a game against the Washington Redskins in 2004. CORBIS

(Top) Miami Dolphins' quarterback Dan Marino grimaces as he is sacked for a loss in a 1999 game against the Indianapolis Colts. CORBIS

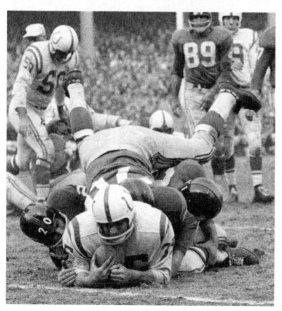

Baltimore Colts' fullback Alan Ameche is buried beneath an avalanche of New York Giants' tacklers in the 1958 NFL title game at Yankee Stadium. The Colts won the game in sudden-death overtime, 23–17. CORBIS

(Left) One of the game's greatest, Jim Brown of the Cleveland Browns, rumbles toward the goal line. JACK ZEHRT

(Below) Kansas City tight end Tony Gonzalez makes a grab. CORBIS

(Below) Jerry Rice making one of his circus catches.

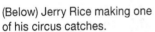

Walter Payton, running back for the Chicago Bears, on the run that broke Jim Brown's rushing record. CORBIS

(Below) Bears' Pro-Bowl linebacker Brian Urlacher tackles New Orleans Saints' running back Deuce McAllister in the 2007 NFC Championship Game. CORBIS

Kansas City kicker Jan Stenerud and quarterback Len Dawson watch as his kick passes through the uprights during Super Bowl IV at Tulane Stadium in New Orleans. The Chiefs would defeat the Minnesota Vikings 23–7. CORBIS

(Bottom) Eli Manning holds up a New York Giants' jersey as he poses with his father (right), former NFL quarterback Archie Manning, his brother Payton Manning, and his mother, Olivia, after Eli was chosen in the 2004 NFL Draft. CORBIS

HALFTIME

TYPICALLY DURING HALFTIME of an NFL telecast, announcers review scores of other games and pour over any number of statistics and numbers to isolate key factors or impending records. Halfway through a book seems like a good time to also do that.

Football isn't the only institution to have a fascination with numbers. So too does the Bible. In fact, it even has a Book of Numbers.

...their whole number was six hundred three thousand five hundred fifty (1:46).

People of biblical times were every bit the statisticians as football fans are today. Certain numbers to the respective faithful immediately call to mind a spiritual passage, Church doctrine, football rule, or record. At the halfway point of our read, I thought we might also pour over the record book and the Good Book for records. Quite often football and faith share the same significant numbers. By no means is the following list to be considered exhaustive, merely indicative.

1

One true God, infinite and eternal, creator of all that is. As Paul wrote to the Corinthians:

Indeed, even though there may be so-called gods in heaven or on earth—as in fact there are many gods and many lords—yet for us there is one God, the Father, from whom are all things and for whom we exist... (1 Corinthians 8:5–6).

One point is what a point after touchdown (PAT) is worth in a football game. Kicked through the uprights from ten yards out after a touchdown has been scored, the PAT is virtually automatic, so much so that people often equate a touchdown with seven points, instead of six. One point is also the difference between winning and losing, a fact made all too painfully obvious to the Buffalo Bills in Super Bowl XXV. After Bills kicker Scott Norwood's 47-yard field goal attempt sailed wide right, Buffalo came up short to the New York Giants, 20–19.

2

A football game is played during two halves. Before the end of each half, the clock is stopped as the two-minute warning is given to both teams. Teams have the option of kicking a point after a touchdown or running or passing for a two-point conversion. Two points are also awarded for a safety, which occurs when a ball carrier is tackled or a quarterback sacked in his own end zone by the defense. Two also is a very comforting number in the Gospel of Matthew. After all, as Jesus states:

"For where two or three are gathered together in my name, I am there among them" (18:20).

3

The Blessed Trinity—Father, Son, and Holy Spirit—the three persons of the one God. As Jesus himself said,

"I have said these things to you while I am still with you. But the Advocate, the Holy Spirit, whom the Father will send in my name, will teach you everything, and remind you of all that I have said to you" (John 14:25–26).

There are also three theological virtues: faith, hope, and charity, which *Life in Christ: A Catholic Catechism for Adults* defines this way: Faith enables us to believe God in whatever he has told us. Hope enables us to have confidence in the forgiveness of sins and eternal life. Love (charity) enables us to love him above all things for his own sake and love ourselves and all people as children of God.[1]

Upon the news of Jesus' birth, Matthew reports a visit from the Magi, thought to be three, from the east, who presented the infant three gifts.

On entering the house, they saw the child with Mary his mother; and they knelt down and paid him homage. Then, opening their treasure chests, they offered him gifts of gold, frankincense, and myrrh (2:11).

From birth to death the number three played a part, for it was on the third day that Christ rose from the dead.

Then he opened their minds to understand the scriptures, and he said to them, "Thus it is written, that the Messiah is to suffer and to rise from the dead the third day, and that repentance and forgiveness of sins is to be proclaimed in his name to all nations..." (Luke 24:45–47).

Three is also the number of points awarded for a field goal. Field goals have played prominently in four Super Bowls. Jim O'Brien kicked a 32-yarder to cap Super Bowl V, giving the Colts a 16–13 victory over the Cowboys. In Super Bowl XXXVI, Adam Vinatieri booted a 48-yarder as time expired giving the Patriots a thrilling win over the St. Louis Rams. Three years later, Vinatieri again provided the margin of victory with a 22-yard FG as the Pats defeated the Eagles 24–21. And as mentioned above, Scott Norwood's missed field goal gave the Giants a victory in Super Bowl XXV against the Bills.

4

In the New Testament, the four gospels of Mark, Matthew, Luke, and John all proclaim in various fashions to different audiences the Good News of the Lord.

There are also four moral virtues, again defined in *Life in Christ*. Fortitude inclines us to do what God desires, even when it is hard and disagreeable. Justice inclines us to give to all persons whatever is properly due to them. Prudence inclines us to form right judgments about what we should and should not do. And temperance inclines us to govern appetite according to what is right and pleasing to God.[2]

Paul's journeys to spread the gospel numbered four. They could conceivably be considered the ultimate road trip. Paul took in the regions of Cyprus, Galatia, Macedonia, Achaia (modern-day Greece), Ephesus, Crete, Malta (where he was shipwrecked), and finally Rome. All this without a traveling secretary, someone to wash his uniform, or a multimillion dollar salary.

Four is an integral number on the gridiron too. There are four quarters to the game. Within each game, possession of the ball is maintained by advancing the leather at least ten yards every four downs. Few plays are more exciting in the last two minutes of a game than fourth down and whatever yards to go to keep a drive alive.

5.2

During the course of his nine-year career, Cleveland Browns running back Jim Brown averaged 5.2 yards per carry—over 2,359 attempts—often with defenses geared to stop him. Brown, on average, gained a first down every two times he touched the ball! These days, a back is considered remarkable if he averages four yards a carry. Not surprisingly, his is the all-time yards-per-carry mark for running backs.

Matthew 5:2 begins one of the most poetic passages of the New Testament. The evangelist recounts the words that Jesus spoke to the multitudes:

> Then he began to speak, and taught them, saying:
> "Blessed are the poor in spirit, for theirs is the kingdom of heaven.
> "Blessed are those who mourn, for they will be comforted.
> "Blessed are the meek, for they will inherit the earth.
> "Blessed are those who hunger and thirst for righteousness, for they will be filled.
> "Blessed are the merciful, for they will receive mercy.
> "Blessed are the pure in heart, for they will see God.
> "Blessed are the peacemakers, for they will be called children of God.
> "Blessed are those who are persecuted for righteousness' sake, for theirs is the kingdom of heaven" (5:2–10).

The beauty of the beatitudes is that they speak to different parts of us all, the reward for which is a place with God in the kingdom of heaven. At different points in our lives, each of us has been gentle, forgiving, or, in the case of Saints' fans, has mourned.

6

As mentioned, a touchdown on the playing field is worth six points. Coincidentally, the most touchdowns scored by the same person in a game is also six, accomplished by Ernie Nevers of the Cardinals

(Chicago edition), Dub Jones of the Browns, and Gale Sayers of the Bears.

Six is the number of days God took to create the cosmos. Recall that the first chapter of Genesis reports that on day one came the heavens and the earth, as well as the separation of light from darkness. Day two brought oceans and sky, while on the third day came dry land, grass, herbs, and fruit trees. The sun and moon appeared on day four, with day five bringing all living creatures. Saving the best for last, God created humankind on day six. At the end of each phase of creation, God looked upon his works and proclaimed, "It's good!"

7

In the Bible, the number seven signifies abundance. And there are plenty of units of seven here, covering everything from sins to sacraments. The former are of the capital, or deadly, variety (anger, covetousness, envy, gluttony, lust, pride, and sloth); the latter being much more full of grace (baptism, reconciliation, Eucharist, confirmation, marriage, holy orders, and the sacrament of the sick).

Referring to *Life in Christ* once again, we discover the seven gifts of the Holy Spirit: wisdom to judge all things as God sees them; understanding with deeper insight the truths God has revealed to us; right judgment to act with prudence; courage to do great things for God; knowledge to see the things of the world in their relation to God; piety to love God as our Father and to have affection for all persons and things; and a fear of the Lord, of offending, and being separated from, him whom we love.[3]

Seven days represent the first week of Creation, including a day of rest to catch NFL games on television. Seven loaves were used to feed the four thousand (Matthew 15:36). Christ taught to forgive seventy-seven times (Matthew 18:22).

Revelation alone could be considered "seven heaven," with references to seven churches, seven golden lamp stands, seven stars, seven Spirits of God, seven lamps of fire, seven seals, seven angels who stand before God, seven trumpets, seven thunders, a red dragon having seven heads, a beast of the sea having seven heads, seven bowls, and seven plagues.

In football, seven of course equals the point total for a touchdown and its corresponding PAT. Seven also is the uniform number of a quarterback who generated a good number of yards. John Elway threw for 51,475 yards, the second largest total ever in the NFL. Equally impressive was the number of times he led the Broncos back from apparent defeat. Forty-seven times Elway directed game-tying or game-winning drives in the fourth quarter, a league best. Now that's abundant!

10

One of the most famous stories in Exodus is of God almighty handing down the Ten Commandments to Moses. Michael Francis Pennock in *The Seeker's Catechism* summarizes the commandments this way[4]:

1. I, the Lord, am your God. You shall not have other gods besides me.
2. You shall not take the name of the Lord, your God, in vain.
3. Remember to keep holy the Sabbath day.
4. Honor your father and your mother.
5. You shall not kill.
6. You shall not commit adultery.
7. You shall not steal.
8. You shall not bear false witness against your neighbor.
9. You shall not covet your neighbor's wife.
10. You shall not covet anything that belongs to your neighbor.

Football, like the Bible, has its fair share of rules and traditions. In football and faith, there are those entrusted with interpreting these guidelines for players and people, fans and faithful alike. Church leaders interpret church rules. In the Catholic Church, the task is performed by priests, they of the starched white collars and black attire. Within the game the job falls to the umpires and referees with their black-and-white zebra shirts and yellow penalty flags.

The ten commandments of football might read:

1. You shall not cross the line of scrimmage until the ball is snapped.
2. You shall not hold to impede a pass rusher's progress.
3. You shall not interfere with a receiver's right to catch a pass.
4. You shall not rough the passer or kicker.
5. You shall not tackle a player by grabbing his facemask.
6. You shall not intentionally throw a pass into the ground to avoid being sacked in the pocket.
7. You shall not initiate contact with an opposing player once the whistle has blown a play dead.
8. Offensive linemen shall not be eligible receivers downfield unless reporting beforehand to an official.
9. You shall not run into the kicker.
10. You shall not taunt an opposing player, nor excessively celebrate a touchdown or sack.

Just as the rules of the game are enforced so that football is played correctly and fairly, so it is with the Ten Commandments. Those directions from God carved in stone and handed to Moses are our rules for the game of life, given to us so that we might be always in right relationship with our Creator and with one another.

On the gridiron, the number ten also plays an important part in every game played. Teams must advance the ball ten yards in four downs in order to gain a first down and repeat the process. If not, as all football fans know, they are usually forced to punt. That a football field is 100 yards long from goal line to goal line further demonstrates the importance of the number ten to the game. It takes 10 ten-yard segments to make up the field.

11

This number represents the original faithful apostles, who followed Jesus, absorbed his teachings as best they could and, after being inflamed by the Holy Spirit at Pentecost, went out to spread the Good News of the Lord. Peter became the rock upon which Christ built his church. Matthew and John recounted the life of Christ in their gospels. James and Jude (sometimes called Thaddeus) wrote epistles encouraging the fledgling Christian communities. Andrew died a martyr; Thomas preached in India. James of Alphaeus (sometimes called James the Lesser so as not to be confused with James, the brother of John), Bartholomew (also known as Nathanael), Simon the Canaanite, and Philip round out Jesus' handpicked team.

Perhaps, in his infinite wisdom, God determined that eleven was the perfect number for a collection of people brought together in pursuit of a common good, such as playing football. Though football teams have rosters that number fifty-three, only eleven players can be on the field at any one time. On offense, these are usually deployed thusly: a center, two guards, two tackles, a tight end, two wide receivers, and one each of full-, half-, and quarterback. On the other side of the ball, defenses typically deploy this way: two defensive tackles, two defensive ends, two cornerbacks, two safeties, and a right, middle, and left linebacker. Occasionally, teams adopt a three-four scheme, meaning three down linemen up front and four linebackers among the first seven.

40

In Genesis, we learn that God instructed Noah to build the ark in preparation for the rain that lasted forty days and forty nights. It took the Israelites forty years to be delivered to the Promised Land. Early in his ministry, Jesus prayed and fasted for forty days; at the end of that time he withstood three temptations by the devil. In the opening of the Acts of the Apostles, we discover that Christ appeared to his disciples for forty days after the resurrection, after which time he ascended into heaven.

One of the most important measurements of a players' athleticism is the 40-yard dash. Any player hoping to be drafted by an NFL team is subjected to a battery of tests, including how many times he can bench press 225 pounds, agility drills, leaping ability, and speed as measured in the 40.

45

This is the number of active players who can dress for any NFL game. Teams are allowed rosters of fifty-three players to be divided up among active participants and those on the practice squad. Think of the names of some of those who have played the game—Brett Favre, Peyton Manning, Emmitt Smith, Bruce Smith, Reggie White, Johnny Unitas, Otto Graham, Joe Montana, Jerry Rice, John Elway, Walter Payton, Barry Sanders, Jim Brown, Dick Butkus, Ray Nitschke, Lawrence Taylor, Deacon Jones—and the last verse of Psalm 45 comes to mind. Though the psalm rejoices in the "marriage" of humanity to Jesus, its closing couplet can easily be applied to all the greats of the gridiron.

> *I will cause your name to be celebrated in all generations;*
> *therefore the peoples will praise you forever and ever*
> (45:17).

99

In his Hall of Fame career, Dallas Cowboy running back Tony Dorsett amassed 16,293 combined yards from rushing and pass-receiving, and 90 touchdowns. Of those totals, 12,739 yards and 77 TDs came from running the football. Of those numbers, 99 yards and a score came on a single play against the Minnesota Vikings in 1983. While that NFL record for the longest run from scrimmage may someday be tied, it will never be broken.

The number ninety-nine is used by Jesus in the parable of the Lost Sheep as a way to contrast the joy in heaven experienced by the repentance of a single sinner.

> *Now all the tax collectors and the sinners were coming near to listen to him. And the Pharisees and scribes were grumbling and saying, "This fellow welcomes sinners and eats with them."*
>
> *So he told them this parable: "Which of you, having a hundred sheep and losing one of them, does not leave the ninety-nine in the wilderness and go after the one that is lost until he finds it? When he has found it, he lays it on his shoulders and rejoices. And when he comes home, he calls together his friends and neighbors, saying to them, 'Rejoice with me, for I have found my sheep that was lost.' Just so, I tell you, there will be more joy in heaven over one sinner who repents than over ninety-nine righteous persons who need no repentance"* (Luke 15:1–7).

This truly is good news for those of us who at times are more like the lost sheep than the faithful members of the flock!

THE IMMACULATES

ONE OF THE MOST FAMOUS PLAYS in all of professional football came on December 23, 1972.

Pittsburgh was hosting the Oakland Raiders in an AFC divisional playoff game at Three Rivers Stadium. The winner would end up playing the undefeated Miami Dolphins for the right to go to the Super Bowl. In a defensive struggle, Oakland held a slim 7–6 lead and the Steelers had their backs against the wall: fourth down, ten yards to go, sixty yards from the goal line, and twenty-two seconds left. Quarterback Terry Bradshaw, seeking enough yardage to set up a game-winning field goal, passed to fullback Frenchy Fuqua at the Raiders 35-yard line.[1] Ball, Fuqua, and hard-hitting Raiders safety Jack Tatum all arrived at the same place at the same time. The force of the Tatum's hit bowled Fuqua over, with the ball careening off one of the players, flying backward in the air. Raiders teammates and fans rejoiced at having apparently escaped with a victory.

Except for one thing.

Steelers running back Franco Harris, a safety valve receiver on the play, had managed to somehow pick the ball out of the air, nanoseconds and millimeters before it hit the ground. Ball tucked safely in his arms, Harris dashed downfield to score the winning touchdown with but five seconds left to play.

Bedlam ensued. Fans rushed the field. Steelers joyously celebrated; Raiders bitterly protested to the officials. And with good reason. Had the ball bounced off Fuqua, Harris would have been ineligible to receive it. At the time, there was no instant replay for the officials on the field to review such a hotly contested play. With no proof to reverse their decision, the officials let the play stand. Extra point made, the Steelers walked off with a miraculous 13–7 victory.

In football lore, the play has become known as the Immaculate Reception, a play itself on the Catholic term *Immaculate Conception*. The phrase was first used on the air by Myron Cope, the Steelers play-by-play announcer. According to Wikipedia, a woman named Sharon Levosky telephoned Cope the night of the game and suggested the term, coined by her friend Michael Ord.[2] No less an authority than NFL Films has chosen the Reception as the greatest play of all time.

As for my memory of it, the play still remains all too clear. As I mentioned earlier, I grew up cheering for both the 49ers and the Raiders, doubling my odds that one of my teams would do well during any football season. In 1971, the 'Niners had moved their home games to Candlestick Park after two decades of playing at Kezar Stadium. So the following season, my dad and I chipped in for 49er season tickets. While a haven for cyclones and fogbanks during night games of the San Francisco Giants, Candlestick was by comparison pleasant and mild for Sunday afternoon football games. Thus, I was hoping for an early Christmas present that year in the guise of 49ers and Raiders playoff triumphs.

As my friend Dennis and I drove to the San Francisco-Dallas NFC divisional playoff game at the 'Stick, we had the Raiders-Steelers game on the car radio. Things looked bleak for the pride and poise boys, trailing 6–0 deep into the fourth quarter. However, Ken Stabler snaked his way downfield for a 30-yard touchdown run, letting Oakland assume a 7–6 lead with only 1:13 left to play. Walking through the parking lot, we felt secure in knowing that once the last twenty-two seconds ticked off the clock in Pittsburgh, the silver-and-black win would be in hand, with only the red-and-gold 49ers victory to go. Passing festive tailgate parties to our right and left, we followed the end of the contest as broadcast on a number of radios tuned to the game.

Suddenly, something went terribly wrong. The order of the cosmos had shifted. An incomplete pass had somehow turned into a Steelers victory, dashing the hopes of Raider Nation, of which I was a member thanks to my dual-football citizenship. I felt a palpable depression take hold of me as I now walked with a heavy heart to my seat among the 49er faithful in the east end zone at Candlestick.

Hope, however, returned in the personage of Vic Washington. No sooner had the Dallas Cowboys kicked off than the 49ers return man ran the ball back 97 yards for a touchdown, giving the home team a quick 7–0 lead. Leave it to the Cowboys, however, to pour salt into my playoff wounds. Cowboy quarterback Roger Staubach entered the game in the fourth quarter to lead Dallas to 17 unanswered points and a miraculous comeback of their own, winning 28–27. I left my heart in San Francisco that day—broken by the red-and-gold fold.

Years later, both the Raiders and 49ers met with a good deal of Super Bowl success, with Oakland winning three titles in seven seasons, and the 'Niners taking home five of the crystal trophies. Consolation and then jubilation had come out of football desolation. And the virtue of patience was practiced for a number of seasons.

Two games, two miraculous finishes. The Immaculate Reception has become part of football history and beyond. A college physics professor has examined the forces in motion in the play to determine which player the ball was most likely to have bounced off of.[3] Frenchy Fuqua knows but he's not telling.[4] Raider fans still feel robbed by the officials' call.

While the play has sparked lively debate and countless discussions, few have gone beyond the events on the field. Yet tremendous meaning and knowledge can be gained by examining the concept that inspired the phrase *Immaculate Reception*.

The *Immaculate Conception*. In the Catholic faith, the Immaculate Conception is one of the most mysterious of beliefs. It's also one of the most misunderstood. Many people, Catholics included, think it refers to the notion of Jesus being conceived in Mary's womb. That event is actually the part of the Incarnation, whereby God assumed human form in Jesus. Catholic Tradition teaches that Jesus was conceived by the Holy Spirit and born of the Virgin Mary. However, the Immaculate Conception refers to the belief that from the instant Mary was first conceived in her mother's womb, she was free from original sin by the grace of God.

To understand the significance of this sinless state, we have to revisit the Book of Genesis. When God discovered that Adam and Eve had eaten of the forbidden fruit, he was none too pleased.

> *To the woman he said:*
> *"I will greatly increase your pangs in childbearing;*
> *in pain you shall bring forth children,*
> *yet your desire shall be for your husband,*
> *and he shall rule over you."*
> *And to the man he said,*
> *"Because you have listened to the voice of your wife,*
> *and have eaten of the tree*
> *about which I commanded you,*
> *'You shall not eat of it,'*
> *cursed is the ground because of you;*
> *in toil you shall eat of it all the days of your life;*
> *thorns and thistles it shall bring forth for you;*
> *and you shall eat the plants of the field.*
> *By the sweat of your face*
> *you shall eat bread*
> *until you return to the ground,*
> *for out of it you were taken;*
> *you are dust,*
> *and to dust you shall return"* (3:16–19).

By their disobedience, Adam and Eve, the first humans, committed the first sin of humanity, the original sin. We have all been stained by it. As the color of eyes and hair is passed down from generation to generation, so is this natural inclination to sin. Fortunately, the sacrament of baptism washes away the stain of original sin. By virtue of the sanctifying grace that accompanies baptism, we gain the forgiveness of sins gained by Christ dying on the cross.

Which brings us back to the Immaculate Conception.

God so loved humanity that he offered his only son as sacrifice for our collective sins. Only by the death of the sinless One, could sin be defeated. Jesus was fully human except for sin. For Jesus to be unstained by sin at birth, his mother would have also had to be unstained by sin. Thus, the Catholic Church believes that Mary must have been without sin from the moment of her own conception—her Immaculate Conception.

For Mary to be born without sin was a miracle. For Franco Harris to catch a pass thrown yards past him and return it for a playoff-clinching victory was also heaven sent, at least according to Pittsburgh Steelers' fans. However, the real wonder of it all comes from the fact that a football play can inspire better understanding of the birth of the Mother of God.

HAIL MARY: FROM PRAYER BOOK TO PLAYBOOK

PRAYER CAN BE DESCRIBED as a quieting of the mind, a refocusing of our hearts on God's purpose for us. Prayer is conversation with our Father. One way to think of our purpose on earth is to be in right relationship with our Creator. As with any relationship, bonds are formed through conversation. Prayers can be offerings of thanksgiving, petitions for solace, praise for life, lamentations of grief, requests for understanding, pleas for guidance, or just a friendly hello. In the Old Testament, one of the traditional forms of prayer was the psalms, poetry that was presented to God in song.

Even Jesus realized the value of prayer. He would often use prayer to refocus his energies on his mission, to reconnect with his father, our God. These times must have been very tender moments between Father and Son, just as our prayers with God can be intimate conversations between Father and child. If the gospels are any indication, there were instances when the Lord felt abandoned and alone, in need of consolation and fortitude.

And after he had dismissed the crowds, he went up to the mountain by himself to pray (Matthew 14:23).

In this case, Jesus had just finished feeding the multitude of five thousand with five loaves and two fish. There are many reasons Christ might have retired to pray. Perhaps preaching to, and feeding, the crowd was emotionally draining. Or maybe he felt flush from the experience or, more likely, pressed upon by the people to do more than he was willing to do at the time. One very real possibility is that the Lord wanted to offer thanks to God for the wonders he was able to work in his Father's name.

In our day and age, think of how besieged an individual is when he or she wins a multimillion-dollar lottery, or how a first-round draft choice is hounded after signing a lucrative pro-football contract. Calls come pouring in from long-lost relatives, childhood friends, passing acquaintances, stockbrokers, charities, real-estate agents, news organizations, companies seeking endorsements, you name it. Now imagine how people would react to someone, who, instead of being able to do wondrous things with a football, could cure illness and disease, make the sick well, heal the mentally disturbed, all with a prayer or a touch of a hand.

> *But now more than ever the word about Jesus spread abroad; many crowds would gather to hear him and to be cured of their diseases. But he would withdraw to deserted places and pray* (Luke 5:15–16).

Though divine, Jesus was also very much human. Plus there are only so many hours in the day. Inevitably, he would have needed to get away if only for a moment's peace of mind, so that he could heal again another day. Jesus repaired to the wilderness. How often have we found a walk in the woods, a stroll along an ocean beach, a mountain hike, or fly-fishing along a scenic river to be revitalizing. As we've seen, God created the skies and the trees and seeds and beasts of the earth. So it's no wonder that God is found in nature. It's also no wonder that the Lord sought him there.

There may come times when we pray for guidance, whether it be in choosing the right career, wondering if a certain someone is our true soul mate, or hoping our team makes a wise decision when choosing among several highly rated players in the NFL draft. In the following passage, Luke suggests that Christ, too, prayed for wisdom the night before his "draft" of the apostles.

> *Now during those days he went out to the mountain to pray; and he spent the night in prayer to God. And when the day came, he called his disciples and chose twelve of them, whom he also named apostles...* (6:12–13).

In a garden the night before he died, the Lord uttered one of his most famous prayers:

> *They went to a place called Gethsemane; and he said to his disciples, "Sit here while I pray." He took with him Peter and James and John, and began to be distressed and agitated. And he said to them, "I am deeply grieved, even to death; remain here, and keep awake." And going a little farther, he threw himself on the ground and prayed that, if it were possible, the hour might pass from him. He said, "Abba, Father, for you all things are possible; remove this cup from me; yet, not what I want, but what you want"* (Mark 14:32–36).

Even Jesus had moments of distress, times of trouble. Was he looking to escape the ordeal and certain death before him? You bet. Did he pray for this petition to be granted? Yes and no. While Christ asked his Father to spare him of what was to come, Jesus knew that we are all here on this earth to do God's will, even if that will may be contrary to our own. So while this prayer was one of petition, it was also one of affirmation of Christ's fidelity to his father.

As with any form of conversation, prayer is equal parts speaking and listening. For most of us, it's easy to do the talking. We ask God for help, forgiveness, understanding, consolation. We give thanks for our children, a sunset, a recovery, a playoff victory. But should we pray to God for guidance of one sort or another, how would we know which way our Father/our Mother would have us turn? This is where quiet meditation and reflective prayer come into play. It is only when we are silent, when we silence the noise around us, that we can hear God's reply. Jesus, the word made flesh, learned how our relationship with the Father would be forged by prayer.

> *"Ask, and it will be given you; search, and you will find; knock, and the door will be opened to you. For everyone who asks receives, and everyone who searches finds, and for everyone who knocks, the door will be opened. Is there anyone among you who, if your child asks for bread, will give a stone? Or if the child asks for a fish, will give a snake? If you then, who are evil, know how to give good gifts to your children, how much more will your Father in heaven give good things to those who ask him!"* (Matthew 7:7–11).

As for how we should lead our lives, Jesus learned of that also.

> *"Therefore do not worry, saying, 'What will we eat?' or 'What will we drink?' or 'What will we wear?' For it is the Gentiles who strive for all these things; and indeed your heavenly Father knows that you need all these things. But strive first for the kingdom of God and his righteousness, and all these things will be given to you as well.*
>
> *"So do not worry about tomorrow, for tomorrow will bring worries of its own. Today's trouble is enough for today"* (Matthew 6:31–34).

> *"But I say to you that listen, Love your enemies, do good to those who hate you, bless those who curse you, pray for*

*those who abuse you....Give to everyone who begs from
you....Do to others as you would have them do to you....*
"Be merciful, just as your Father is merciful" (Luke
6:27–28, 30–31, 36).

One of the most popular prayers in all of the Catholic faith is the
Hail Mary. Its opening phrase—Hail Mary, full of grace—speaks
to her favored status with God and alludes to the state of her birth,
her Immaculate Conception.

Examining the prayer reveals that it is composed of three parts,
with Scripture inspiring the first two sections. "Hail Mary, full of
grace, the Lord is with thee, blessed art thou among women" finds
its roots from the angel Gabriel's greeting in Luke 1:28. "And blessed
is the fruit of thy womb, Jesus" comes from Elizabeth's greeting to
Mary as described in Luke 1:42. Completing the prayer is a petition—"Holy Mary, Mother of God, pray for us sinners now, and
at the hour of our death. Amen"—ascribed to the Council of Trent,
an ecumenical meeting of Church leaders in the sixteenth century.[1]
Little did Luke and the council members know that they would help
define a staple of football playbooks everywhere.

Typically, a "Hail Mary pass" is one where the wide receivers
go long, the quarterback flings the football as far as he can, the
defensive backs try to knock it down, and the receivers try to either
leap high and catch it or grab it off the deflection before it hits the
ground. Usually the pass is called when the offensive team is down
to its last play and last resort. The pass is so named because the odds
of completing it are so low that most people feel divine intervention
is needed for success.

While the term had been around for years, Cowboys quarterback
Roger Staubach is given credit for popularizing it. In a 1975 NFC
playoff game, Dallas was near defeat at the hands of the Minnesota
Vikings, down 14–10 with only thirty-six seconds remaining. The
stage: ball on the fifty-yard line, fourth down and sixteen yards
needed to keep the Dallas drive alive. Staubach heaved a desperation

pass toward the end zone. Wideout Drew Pearson, tightly covered by Vikings Nate Wright, had to come back for the slightly underthrown pass. In the tussle for the ball, Pearson was able to pin it to his right hip, and tiptoe down the sideline for the winning touchdown. When recounting the amazing play, the Dallas QB said he closed his eyes, threw the ball as far as he could, and said a Hail Mary.[2]

Undoubtedly, the most famous Hail Mary pass, and the one that imbedded the term in people's memories, came compliments of Boston College quarterback Doug Flutie and his favorite receiver, Gerard Phelan. Playing in a sold-out Orange Bowl the day after Thanksgiving in 1984, the Golden Eagles of Boston were involved in a scoring shootout with the defending national champion Miami Hurricanes. With six seconds left on the clock, on the last play of the game, Flutie heaved a 48-yard bomb (actually the ball traveled 60 yards in the air) toward the Miami end zone where three of his receivers would try to either catch the pass or tip it to a teammate. Hurricanes and Eagles players bunched up near the goal line, not thinking the five-foot nine-inch Flutie had the arm strength to reach touchdown territory. Phelan had slipped behind the defenders just as the ball came down and caught it as time ran out, giving BC a 47–45 come-from-behind win.[3] The stature of the game, sold-out Orange Bowl, and holiday national television audience all added to the mystique of the play. All that night and the next day sports shows replayed highlights of the answered prayer; all around the country it was the lead story in the next day's sports sections.

In all the excitement about these plays and several like them, one question begs further study: What is it about the Hail Mary that makes it such a powerful prayer that even football teams will call upon it?

The answers lie in the prayer itself.

First, there is incredible wonder in the phrase, "The Lord is with you." Five short words, yet so full of meaning. At the annunciation, when the angel Gabriel first tells Mary of her special status, the holy messenger reveals that the Lord God is with her. Not that God will be with her when the time comes to conceive, but is with her now. And has been with her always. This is much the same notion as when God described himself to Moses at the burning bush:

"*I AM WHO I AM*" (Exodus 3:14).

I AM WHO has always been. I AM WHO will always be. I AM WHO always is. Similarly, when Gabriel says to Mary that, "The Lord is with you," he is stating emphatically that God has always been with Mary and will always be with Mary. God is constantly with Mary in the ever-present now.

Gabriel goes on to say:

"*Do not be afraid, Mary, for you have found favor with God*" (Luke 1:30).

From the first part of the Hail Mary, it is not hard to see why Catholics believe that she was immaculately conceived. Mary, as the woman who gave birth to the son of God became the mother of God. As the only fully human being to be without sin, as the mother of God, she holds a special place in Catholic teaching and in heaven above.

Not surprisingly, she held a special place in her son's heart too.

On the third day there was a wedding in Cana of Galilee, and the mother of Jesus was there. Jesus and his disciples had also been invited to the wedding. When the wine gave out, the mother of Jesus said to him, "They have no wine." And Jesus said to her, "Woman, what concern is that to you and to me? My hour has not yet come." His mother said to the servants, "Do whatever he tells you." Now standing there were six stone water jars for the Jewish rites of purification, each holding twenty or thirty gallons. Jesus said to them, "Fill the jars with water." And they filled them up to the brim. He said to them, "Now draw some out, and take it to the chief steward." So they took it. When the steward tasted the water that had become wine, and did not know where it came from (though the servants who had drawn the water knew), the steward called the bridegroom and said to him, "Everyone serves the good wine first, and then the inferior wine after the guests have become drunk. But you have kept the good wine until now." Jesus did this, the first of his signs, in Cana of Galilee, and revealed his glory; and his disciples believed in him (John 2:1–11).

From John's Gospel, we learn a number of things. Yes, Jesus knew his way around fine wine. But more importantly, this passage exemplifies the respect and love Christ had for his mother. From his remarks it is clear he does not consider this wedding feast to be the time nor the place to begin his ministry, and certainly not the occasion for his first miracle. As with most kids, he tried to reason with his mom. Using a term of respectful address, Jesus attempted to dissuade Mary from involving him. Yet when she pressed on in order to help the newly married couple avoid a potentially embarrassing social situation, Jesus obediently, dutifully, respectfully complied.

And then some.

Jesus turned water into somewhere between 120 and 180 gallons of the finest wine, roughly 600 to 900 bottles of a vintage far superior than the best wine the wedding couple could provide. He demonstrated power over nature and gave an example of how he could transform. In so doing, Christ indicated what was to come: his transformation of our transgressions by his forgiveness, his overcoming death with life. He showed a son's love and respect for his mother.

With this in mind, it's not surprising that the Council of Trent concluded the Hail Mary with the petition mentioned earlier: "Holy Mary, Mother of God, pray for us sinners now and at the hour of our death. Amen." Think of it. God has been with Mary forever;

she has found favor with the Almighty. Jesus, the Son of God, the savior of the world, the son of man, paradoxically 100 percent human and 100 percent divine, listened to his mother and honored her requests. Mary is our intercessor, our go-between. Who else better to put in a good word for us when God is calling us home?

The Catholic Church thinks so highly of Mary that it created the rosary as a way to honor her. Often prayed with a set of beads, the rosary is a collection of meditative prayers including the Apostles' Creed, Our Father, Hail Mary, and Glory to the Father. As a set of prayers, it is a powerful expression of faith.

By saying the Apostles' Creed, Catholics state their beliefs in the Father, Son, and Holy Spirit; salvation by the death and resurrection of Jesus; the forgiveness of sins, the cleansing power of baptism. The Our Father contains one of the most powerful expressions of hope in all the gospels:

> *Your kingdom come.*
> *Your will be done,*
> *on earth as it is in heaven* (Matthew 6:10).

No matter how sad or tragic things may appear in our lives, regardless of the man-made wars that rage or the natural disasters that destroy, God's plan will prevail.

As discussed, the Hail Mary entreats the mother of God to be with us in our hours of need. Finally, the Glory to the Father allows us the opportunity to offer praise to the Father, Son, and Spirit.

Chances are Mary does not become actively involved in the outcomes of football games, no matter how big a fan she may be. Yet, when teams are faced with dire circumstances, they realize that without some special help from somewhere, they may not have the resources to win. Faced with illness, the loss of a loved one, financial difficulty, addictions, family strife, we too realize that we may not have the will or the skills to endure. That's why in both football and faith, we offer up a prayer to Mary, to Jesus, to God, not necessarily to affect an outcome, but to seek the strength to accept whatever that outcome may be. We realize that, despite our sometimes stubborn natures, we cannot exist without God's love, care, protection, forgiveness, and grace.

In our minds we may pray, "Holy Mary, Mother of God, pray for us sinners now and at the hour of our death" and when we need a 50-yard touchdown pass with three seconds left on the clock, "Amen." But in our hearts, we know better. We pray, "Thank you for listening to us Mary, thank you for forgiving us Jesus, thank you for loving us God. May we do the same for others."

Amen!

GENTILES AND THE AMERICAN FOOTBALL LEAGUES

SINCE ITS INCEPTION IN 1920, first as the American Professional Football Association and later as the National Football League, the NFL had been threatened by rival leagues. In 1926, when the Chicago Bears refused to pay Red Grange a five-figure salary and give him one-third ownership of the team, Grange became the focal point of a new league: the first American Football League. Grange played for the AFL's New York Yankees. In the league's inaugural season, the Philadelphia Quakers claimed the championship. Unfortunately, the AFL's first season was also its final one. No doubt fans became disappointed in the caliber of play, as evidenced by the 31–0 pasting of the AFL champion Quakers by the NFL Giants in an end-of-season game.[1] It should be noted that these were the seventh-place NFL Giants.

Even though the NFL was having its ups (twenty-two franchises in 1926) and downs (ten teams two years later), it at least had some semblance of stability. Not so for its rivals. In 1936, another American Football League was formed. This one was twice as successful as its predecessor, which meant it produced a pair of champions—the Boston Shamrocks and Los Angeles Bulldogs. It folded in two years.[2]

In 1940, a new six-team affiliation was born. With great imagination, they called themselves the American Football League. The Columbus Bullies lived up to their name, bullying the other five teams to win back-to-back titles. That was all they would win as this version of the AFL also packed it in after two seasons.[3]

It wasn't until 1946 that a league burst upon the scene with any sort of staying power. Learning from their three predecessors, these eight teams did not call themselves the American Football League. This alone may have been sufficient to ensure their success. As the All-America Football Conference, this latest competition to the NFL proved to be legitimate, led by Paul Brown's Cleveland Browns and their incredible quarterback Otto Graham. In fact, the level of play was so high that three of the AAFC teams were invited to join the National Football League: the four-time champion Cleveland Browns, the 1949 title-game playing San Francisco 49ers, and the Baltimore Colts (who disbanded after only one NFL season).[4] It is important to note that while three teams were chosen to join the senior league, the remaining AAFC franchises were not.

Fast-forward to 1960 and the formation of yet another American Football League with some familiar sounding names: Boston Patriots, Buffalo Bills, Dallas Texans, Denver Broncos, Houston Oilers, Los Angeles Chargers, New York Titans, and Oakland Raiders.[5] With sound financial backing and star players of its own—George Blanda, Clem Daniels, Len Dawson, Ron Mix, and Lance Alworth—this AFL gathered fan support and legitimacy. With each new season, the league's popularity grew. New champions were born with Houston (twice), Dallas, Boston, San Diego (new home of the Chargers), and Buffalo (twice) taking home the league crown.

With both NFL and AFL seeking to sign the same college players, salaries escalated, threatening the financial stability of the sport. Both leagues reached the same conclusion: If you can't outspend 'em, join 'em. Thus, the NFL and entire AFL merged, creating one big happy football family. As mentioned, the subsequent NFL-AFL championship game became known as the Super Bowl. And the rest is Roman numeral history.

What's surprising about these developments is that they parallel the formation of the early Church. As noted, the NFL was exclusionary with regard to other teams and leagues. So too were the early followers of Christ with regard to Gentiles. For a while even Jesus had limited the audience of his ministry. With time, and insight, both the Lord and his followers expanded their thinking to be all-inclusive. Just like the NFL.

Early Christianity was a closed society. From the time God made his covenant with Abraham, the Jews believed themselves to be the Chosen People. Prophets such as Isaiah predicted the coming of Christ to God's people, with two of the most famous of proclamations being these:

"*Look, the young woman is with child and shall bear a son, and shall name him Immanuel*" (Isaiah 7:14).

> *For a child has been born for us,*
> *a son given to us...*
> *and he is named*
> *Wonderful, Counselor, Mighty God,*
> *Everlasting Father, Price of Peace* (Isaiah 9:6).

Jesus was born a Jew, no doubt studied the Torah, taught and preached in the temple. His handpicked followers were Jewish, as were most of those to whom they ministered. As such, the foundations of what eventually became Catholicism and Christianity were decidedly Jewish. In fact, "the Way" of the Lord was considered by many to be a small sect within the Jewish faith. However, it was a woman, and a Gentile at that, who helped influence Jesus to expand his thinking about his mission.

From there he set out to the region of Tyre. He entered a house and did not want anyone to know he was there.

> *Yet he could not escape notice, but a woman whose little daughter had an unclean spirit immediately heard about him, and she came and bowed down at his feet. Now the woman was a Gentile, of Syrophoenician origin. She begged him to cast the demon out of her daughter. He said to her, "Let the children be fed first, for it is not fair to take the children's food and throw it to the dogs." But she answered him, "Sir, even the dogs under the table eat the children's crumbs." Then he said to her, "For saying that, you may go—the demon has left your daughter." So she went home, found the child lying on the bed, and the demon gone* (Mark 7:24–30).

In his mind, Jesus' first priority was to minister to his "children," the sheep of Israel. Thus, a Greek woman would not normally command his attention. But through their playful verbal sparring, a remarkable thing happened—a shift in Jesus' thinking, a change of the Lord's heart. All people, Jew and Gentile alike, could benefit from the word of God.

In John's Gospel, Jesus broke open his word for a Samaritan woman at a time when Jews and Samaritans were as friendly as the Jews and Palestinians of today. In Matthew's Gospel, Jesus reached out beyond his Jewish audience to a Roman centurion, a rather bold move since Judea was under Roman rule at the time. In effect, Jesus was opening up his heart to the Jews' oppressors.

From the Gentile woman to the Roman centurion, Jesus is genuinely pleased, perhaps even astounded, that great faith could be found outside the Chosen People. Yet, despite Christ's example of reaching out to Jews, Gentiles, Romans, and Samaritans alike, his apostles were not exactly quick studies. His early followers, including Peter, the Rock, the new leader of the fledgling faith community, had been preaching the good news of the Lord only to the Jews. It wasn't until Peter had received a vision housed in a strange dream that he expanded his thinking to include Gentiles.

"We are witnesses to all that he did both in Judea and Jerusalem. They put him to death by hanging him on a tree; but God raised him on the third day and allowed him to appear, not to all the people but to us who were chosen by God as witnesses, and who ate and drank with him after he rose from the dead...."

While Peter was still speaking, the Holy Spirit fell upon all who heard the word. The circumcised believers who had come with Peter were astounded that the gift of the Holy Spirit had been poured out even on the Gentiles, for they heard them speaking in tongues and extolling God....

...And they praised God, saying, "Then God has given even to the Gentiles the repentance that leads to life" (Acts of the Apostles 10:39–41, 44–46; 11:18).

Jews and Gentiles are both to be included in the coming kingdom. Can you say "merger"?

A TALE OF TWO PAULS

IN ITS EARLY DAYS, football was considered "three yards and a cloud of dust," a description of a short-yardage running play and the dirty upheaval caused with the subsequent tackle. It wasn't until 1906, nearly twenty-five years after football had been formally played, that the forward pass was introduced. It wasn't until forty years later when Paul Brown came along that the passing game and offenses really took off.

As a high-school coach in Ohio, Brown had made the first of several names for himself. At one point his team had won fifty-eight of sixty games. His innovative approach to the game earned him the head-coaching job with Ohio State, where he brought the Buckeyes their first national championship in 1942. When Cleveland formed its professional football team for the All-America Football Conference, there was really only one man in Ohio suited to coach the team—Paul Brown. He was so respected in fact that when the Cleveland *Plain Dealer* conducted a readership poll as to what the new team should be called, the winning name was the Browns.[1]

As mentioned previously, the Browns under Brown's leadership won ten conference or league titles in ten years, including four AAFC crowns and three NFL championships. One could say that the AAFC Browns ran the NFL Cleveland Rams out of town, outdrawing them in attendance early on before the Rams moved to Los Angeles. In Brown's seventeen years of coaching the Cleveland team bearing his name, he had only one losing season.

Part of Brown's success stemmed from the fact that he was a

student of the game and also a teacher. Thus, he brought a number of firsts to the way pro football was played. For instance, he instituted a scouting system that utilized a scale for rating players. He used intelligence tests to gauge a player's learning ability. He brought notebooks, classroom sessions, and film study to the game. By rotating two guards in and out on alternating plays, he brought play-calling from the sideline to the huddle. Brown pursued African American players such as now Hall of Famers Marion Motley and Bill Willis.[2] He even was the first to place facemasks on helmets, thereby pleasing the wives of NFL players while at the same time disappointing team dentists.

With his attention to detail, he developed pass routes that were designed to isolate weaknesses in the opposing team's defense, alternately devising defenses that had no such holes. Today, football fans regularly regard former 49ers coach Bill Walsh as an offensive genius, the orchestrator of the West Coast Offense. Walsh was a protégé of Paul Brown.[3]

Not only did Brown bring fame and championships to Cleveland, he brought pro football to Cincinnati. A dispute with owner Art Model ended Brown's tenure with Cleveland. However, when the Bengals joined the NFL in 1967, Paul Brown was not only the coach but also part owner. Even with castoffs and rejects from other teams forming much of Cincy's roster, Brown led them to the playoffs in three of the eight years he coached the team, including their first appearance in only their third year of operation.[4]

As a tribute to his influence on the game, two football stadiums bear his name: Paul Brown Tiger Stadium in Massillon, Ohio, and Paul Brown Stadium in Cincinnati, home of the Bengals. What's more, years after the Cleveland franchise moved to Baltimore to become the Ravens, Cleveland gained an expansion team of their own, appropriately and rightfully named the Browns.

Just as football has its innovators to advance the game, so too does the Christian faith. If Jesus was the founder and CEO of Christianity, then Saint Paul was his director of marketing. More than anyone else, Paul was responsible for spreading the gospel throughout the Mediterranean. His four journeys brought news of the death and resurrection of Jesus to much of the then-European world, including what is now Turkey, Greece, and Italy.

Most Christians and Catholics know the story of Saul's/Paul's conversion. It is one of the more dramatic tales of the Acts of the Apostles.

> Meanwhile Saul, still breathing threats and murder against the disciples of the Lord, went to the high priest and asked him for letters to the synagogues at Damascus, so that if he found any who belonged to the Way, men or women, he might bring them bound to Jerusalem. Now as he was going along and approaching Damascus, suddenly a light from heaven flashed around him. He fell to the ground and heard a voice saying to him, "Saul, Saul, why do you persecute me?" He asked, "Who are you, Lord?" The reply came, "I am Jesus, whom you are persecuting. But get up and enter the city and you will be told what you are to do...."
>
> But the Lord said to him, "Go, for [Saul] is an instrument whom I have chosen to bring my name before Gentiles and kings and before the people of Israel" (9:1–6, 15–16).

Some may feel that Paul's encounter with the Son of God makes for great storytelling but is lacking in the area of historical accuracy. Yet how often does God knock us off our own horse? It may be the loss of a job, a serious illness, the death of a loved one, the devastation caused by a natural disaster, a diagnosis of cancer. It may even be something as glorious as the birth of a child or a once-in-a-lifetime sunset. At some point in our lives, something will cause us to wake up, to see God and our relationship with him in a new light. In so doing all of our words and deeds, thoughts and actions, from that point forward will take on new meaning.

In Paul's case, he traveled as an itinerant tentmaker by day and evangelist by night, so to speak. He not only formed small communities, he wrote them letters, called epistles, to encourage, admonish, and guide members in their newfound faith. Paul's letters are still instructive to this day.

In his Letter to the Romans, Paul speaks of the individual gifts we've been given and how we must share these with one another and work together for the good of all.

> ...each according to the measure of faith that God has assigned. For as in one body we have many members, and not all the members have the same function, so we, who are many, are one body in Christ, and individually we are members one of another. We have gifts that differ according to the grace given to us: prophecy, in proportion to faith; ministry, in ministering; the teacher, in teaching; the exhorter, in exhortation; the giver, in generosity; the leader, in diligence; the compassionate, in cheerfulness (12:3–8).

In Paul's First Letter to the Corinthians, he expands on this theme, showing how out of diversity should come unity.

> Now there are varieties of gifts, but the same Spirit; and there are varieties of services, but the same Lord; and there are varieties of activities, but it is the same God who activates all of them in everyone. To each is given the manifestation of the Spirit for the common good. To one is given through the Spirit the utterance of wisdom, and to another the utterance of knowledge according to the same Spirit, to another faith by the same Spirit, to another gifts of healing by the one Spirit, to another the working of miracles, to another prophecy, to another the discernment of spirits, to another various kinds of tongues, to another the interpretation of tongues. All these are activated by one and the same

Spirit, who allots to each one individually just as the Spirit chooses (12:4–11).

I expect that Paul would be a Vikings fan. After all, the purple and white play in the area of Minneapolis and St. Paul. As a fan of the game, Paul might have also said, "There are varieties of talents, but from the same Spirit. There are varieties of skills, but from the same Lord. And there are varieties of positions, but it is the same God who works all in all. To each is given through the manifestation of the Spirit for the common good of the team: for to one is given the ability to throw the football accurately great distances, to another the acrobatic skill to catch such passes, to another gifts to block, to another the working of miracles in playoff games against the Raiders, to another the talent to punt a ball high and far, to another to kick the ball through goal posts, to another different kinds of running ability, to another the ability to tackle and sack quarterbacks. All these are activated by one and the same Spirit who gives to each one individually as the Spirit chooses."

It is through God-given gifts and the human capacity for hard work that football players perfect their talents. It is by coming together as highly skilled individuals and working together as a team that championships are won. It is also by our own gifts and hard work, as well as coming together as a community, that good things happen—the building of a school, the adoption of orphans, the dedication of a state park, the volunteering for Habitat for Humanity, the supporting of those who have lost loved ones through military service.

For all his admonishments and adventures, his preaching and teachings, Paul proved to be very human. Before traveling the road to Damascus, he had been on a wayward path. As a Roman citizen and Jewish Pharisee, he became hell-bent on persecuting any Jews who had "defected" to follow the way of the Lord. As Luke said in Acts, Paul breathed threats and murder against the disciples. At the very least he served as a bounty hunter, persecuting early Christians and delivering them to prison. That God could call on such a one to be his voice to the masses and, later on, in the Masses, should give hope to all of us.

Still, even with his conversation with Jesus, his miraculous conversion, his direct insight as to what Jesus asked of him and us, Paul realized that it was much easier said than done.

> *For we know that the law is spiritual; but I am of the flesh, sold into slavery under sin. I do not understand my own actions. For I do not do what I want, but I do the very thing I hate. Now if I do what I do not want, I agree that the law is good. But in fact it is no longer I that do it, but sin that dwells within me. For I know that nothing good dwells within me, that is, in my flesh. I can will what is right, but I cannot do it. For I do not do the good I want, but the evil I do not want is what I do. Now if I do what I do not want, it is no longer I that do it, but sin that dwells within me* (Romans 7:14–20).

Moses, David, Peter, Paul. All had their share of sins against humanity. Add to that list you and me. Being human, we tend to err. Fortunately, Jesus, by his death and resurrection, has overcome sin, forever allowing us to seek mercy from the Father. Just as Moses, David, Peter, and Paul sinned, they were also called by God for so much more: to lead the Jews out of captivity, to be a patriarch of the forbearers of Christ, to be the rock upon which the Church was built, to bring the word of God to the world at large. Our task is to learn to listen for God's call to us, so that we too will be able to do great things in the name of the Lord.

In one of the most read and most poetic passages of the Bible, Paul points the way as to how we should act in order to live up to the potential of God in each of us. Take your time with it. It is quite possibly the most valuable lesson in this book.

If I speak in the tongues of mortals and of angels, but do not have love, I am a noisy gong or a clanging cymbal. And if I have prophetic powers, and understand all mysteries and all knowledge, and if I have all faith, so as to remove mountains, but do not have love, I am nothing. If I give away all my possessions, and if I hand over my body so that I may boast, but do not have love, I gain nothing.

Love is patient; love is kind; love is not envious or boastful or arrogant or rude. It does not insist on its own way; it is not irritable or resentful; it does not rejoice in wrongdoing, but rejoices in the truth. It bears all things, believes all things, hopes all things, endures all things.

Love never ends. But as for prophecies, they will come to an end; as for tongues, they will cease; as for knowledge, it will come to an end. For we know only in part, and we prophesy only in part; but when the complete comes, the partial will come to an end. When I was a child, I spoke like a child. I thought as a child, I reasoned like a child; when I became an adult, I put an end to childish ways. For now we see in a mirror, dimly, but then we will see face to face. Now I know only in part; then I will know fully, even as I have been fully known. And now faith, hope, and love abide, these three; and the greatest of these is love (1 Corinthians 13:1–13).

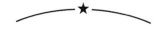

OH, 'DEM SAINTS

AS ANY FAN IN THE STANDS or member of the faithful in the pews knows, football and Christianity have their fair share of saints. And we can learn valuable lessons from both varieties.

As for the NFL kind, perhaps the most famous was Archie Manning, beloved quarterback and 1978 NFC Man of the Year. Though his statistics don't compare with some of the all-time greats at his position, Manning may have posted the most impressive stats of any Saints player, past or present. Often playing behind an offensive line that was overmatched at best and porous at worst, the former Ole Miss star was one of the most-sacked quarterbacks of all time. That he was constantly pressured no doubt contributed to his 171 interceptions. In spite of constant defensive harassment, Manning scrambled and improvised enough to pass for 23,911 yards in his career for 125 touchdowns. Though he played ten NFL seasons, he never had a winning one. Still, he was a two-time All-Pro and the NFL Player of the Year in 1978.

What many people don't realize is that Archie Manning was born Elisha Archibald Manning III.[1] What many people also don't realize is that Elisha was one of the most well-known Old Testament prophets.

Mentored by the great prophet Elijah, Elisha began his ministry around 850 BC. His exploits are chronicled in the Second Book of Kings, which deals with the history of one Jewish people inhabiting two kingdoms, Judah and Israel. What's noteworthy about Elisha's life is that he either duplicated or prefigured a number of miracles that occurred in both the Old and New Testaments.

He took the mantle of Elijah that had fallen from him, and struck the water, saying,

> *"Where is the LORD, the God of Elijah?" When he had struck the water, the water was parted to the one side and to the other, and Elisha went over (2 Kings 2:14).*

Elisha's parting of the Jordan River was identical to Elijah doing the same and reminiscent of Moses parting the Sea of Reeds in leading the Israelites out of captivity from Egypt. By being able to do so, Elisha was shown to be a true and faithful prophet of God like those before him, for none of the men could have worked wonders of their own accord, only by the work of the Father through them.

Two of Christ's most memorable miracles to come were referenced by Elisha. In the first, the prophet caused a widow's jar to produce an endless supply of oil so that the woman would be able to sell the liquid so she and her sons could live. This is reminiscent of Jesus feeding a crowd of five thousand men plus women and children with five loaves and two fish as described in the gospels of Matthew, Mark, and Luke. In each case, God provided much from little. When we put the will of God first, he will care for our needs.

> *As [Jesus] went ashore, he saw a great crowd; and he had compassion for them, because they were like sheep without a shepherd; and he began to teach them many things. When it grew late, his disciples came to him and said, "This is a deserted place, and the hour is now very late; send them away so that they may go into the surrounding country and villages and buy something for themselves to eat." But he answered them, "You give them something to eat." They said to him, "Are we to go and buy two hundred denarii worth [two hundred days' worth of labor] of bread, and give it to them to eat?" And he said to them, "How many*

loaves have you? Go and see." When they found out, they said, "Five, and two fish." Then he ordered them to get all the people to sit down in groups on the green grass. So they sat down in groups of hundreds and of fifties. Taking the five loaves and two fish, he looked up to heaven, and blessed and broke the loaves, and gave them to his disciples to set before the people; and he divided the two fish among them all. And all ate and were filled....Those who had eaten the loaves numbered five thousand men (Mark 6:34–42, 44).

Later in 2 Kings, by raising the Shunammite woman's son from the dead, Elisha set the stage, so to speak, for Jesus' most famous miracle.

When Jesus arrived, he found that Lazarus had already been in the tomb four days....When Martha heard that Jesus was coming, she went and met him, while Mary stayed at home. Martha said to Jesus, "Lord if you had been here, my brother would not have died. But even now I know that God will give you whatever you ask of him...."

Then Jesus, again greatly disturbed, came to the tomb. It was a cave, and a stone was lying against it. Jesus said, "Take away the stone." Martha, the sister of the dead man, said to him, "Lord, already there is a stench because he has been dead for four days." Jesus said to her, "Did I not tell you that if you believed, you would see the glory of God?" So they took away the stone. And Jesus looked upward and said, "Father I thank you for having heard me. I knew that you always hear me, but I have said this for the sake of the crowd standing here, so that they may believe that you sent me." When he had said this, he cried with a loud voice, "Lazarus, come out!" The dead man came out, his hands and feet bound with strips of cloth, and his face wrapped in a cloth, Jesus said to them, "Unbind him and let him go" (John 11:17, 20–22, 38–44).

Here Jesus accomplished the unfathomable—raising a man from the dead. In doing so, Christ revealed heartfelt emotion. He was so overcome he groaned. John says *Jesus began to weep. So the Jews said, "See how he loved him!"* (John 11:35). They may have been tears of grief that Christ wept for his friend and sisters. They may have been tears of sadness that, as a human, Lazarus would have to face death again. Perhaps Jesus was anticipating his own death. Or the fact that it had come to this, after all the words he had preached and the works he had performed, there were still those with him who doubted his ministry.

Regardless, as he had done time and again, Jesus called upon the love of his Father and performed the miracle of miracles. True, modern medicine has allowed doctors to resuscitate victims who have been technically dead in that their hearts had stopped. But Lazarus had been pronounced dead, wrapped in burial clothes, and entombed for four days! In earlier miracles, Jesus had demonstrated power over nature, the elements, sickness, handicaps, and now death itself. The stage was set for his own death—and the overcoming of it by his resurrection.

While perhaps not of the same category of a miracle, it is rather remarkable that a New Orleans Saints quarterback can provide the connection to a prophet of the Old Testament who performed signs predicting the wonders of what was to come by way of the Son of God, Jesus Christ. Whoda thunk it?

Among the more famous saints of the Christian sort are Saint Francis of Assisi, Joan of Arc, Saint Jude, Saint Patrick, Saint Clair, Saint Rose of Lima, and Saint Thomas Aquinas. Just as with Saint Manning, we can learn life lessons from these holy but human individuals.

Though born of a wealthy family, Saint Francis took a vow of poverty at age twenty. In the early 1200s he established the Franciscan Order, still in existence today. As a sign of his devotion to God, Francis was gifted with the stigmata; that is, he physically retained on his hands and feet the wounds of Christ on the cross. With a delicate simplicity, one of the most hopeful prayers in all of Christianity is attributed to Francis. Appropriately titled the Prayer of Saint Francis, it reads:

> Lord, make me an instrument of your peace.
> > where there is hatred, let me sow love;
> > where there is injury, pardon;
> > where there is doubt, faith;
> > where there is despair, hope;
> > where there is darkness, light;
> > and where there is sadness, joy.
>
> O, Divine Master,
> > grant that I may not so much seek
> > to be consoled as to console;
> > to be understood as to understand;
> > to be loved as to love.
>
> For it is in giving that we receive;
> > it is in pardoning that we are pardoned;
> > and it is dying that we are born to eternal life.[2]

As a teenager, Joan of Arc led the French to victory over the English in the Hundred Years' War. Instead of being proclaimed a national heroine, she was branded a heretic and burned at the stake.

A relative of Jesus, Saint Jude Thaddeus had the misfortune to have a name similar to that of Judas, the apostle who betrayed Christ. Thus, many early Christians ignored him and devotion to him became something of a lost cause. As patron saint of lost or impossible causes, Saint Jude is one of the most revered saints (and one of my mom's favorites). Here is the Prayer to Saint Jude because at some time in our lives we just may face an impossible cause of our own.

> Most holy apostle, Saint Jude, faithful servant and friend of Jesus, the name of the traitor who delivered your beloved

Master into the hands of his enemies has caused you to be forgotten by many, but the Church honors and invokes you universally as the patron of hopeless causes, of things almost despaired of. Come to my assistance in this great need that I may receive the consolation and help of heaven in all my necessities, tribulations, and sufferings, particularly *(add your own request here)* and that I may praise God with you and all the elect forever. I promise, O blessed Saint Jude, to be ever mindful of this great favor, to always honor you as my special and powerful patron, and to gratefully encourage devotion to you. Amen.[3]

Many people are familiar with the story of Saint Patrick, given the celebration of his feast day, often with green beer (and in New York a green line painted down Fifth Avenue). Using a shamrock to explain the concept of the Blessed Trinity, Patrick is responsible for converting virtually all of Ireland from Druidism to Christianity in the fifth century. What many don't know is that Patrick wasn't Irish. Though he spoke Celtic, Saint Patrick was born in Scotland![4]

Known to teammates as "The Geek," Robert "Bob" Bruce St. Clair was famous for sacrificing his body so that others might gain. So often and well did the six-foot nine-inch St. Clair do this, that three of his San Francisco contemporaries—Hugh McIlhenny, Joe Perry, and John Henry Johnson—were enshrined. Ten times alone in 1956 did St. Clair block the enemy's attempted field goals. Once when blocking a punt he lost five of his teeth. He made the Hall of Fame in 1990. Later in life, St. Clair undertook a life of service as Mayor of Daly City, California.[5]

Born Isabel in Lima, Peru, in 1586, Saint Rose received her name by way of her parents who thought she was such a treasure they called her their Rose. Obedient as a child, she did all her parents asked of her except marry, preferring to devote her life to God. So that people would not be distracted by her beauty, she often rubbed pepper on her face until her skin blistered, dressed in shabby clothes, and cut her hair. Known for offering her suffering to God, she is, to no surprise, the patron saint of florists.[6]

Saint Thomas Aquinas was born into a family of nobility and wealth. Living in Italy in the 1200s, his could have been a life of leisure and pleasure. Instead he chose a life dedicated to academia and holiness. His family was so upset that they kidnapped him, keeping him under house arrest for more than a year with the hopes of changing his mind. They even tempted him with beautiful women! All to no avail. As a doctor of theology, Thomas authored his *Summa Theologica* rather than become Archbishop of Naples. This compendium of spiritual thinking is considered one of the inspirational cornerstones of Christian faith.[7]

Too often we think of saints as being extremely holy, devoted, pious men and women willing to die for their faith. And for a good many, this was indeed the case. But there were those who showed very real signs of humanity too. Saint Peter was headstrong and denied Jesus three times. Saint Thomas doubted that Christ rose from the dead. Saint Augustine had an illicit affair and bore a son out of wedlock. Yet each overcame their flaws to live remarkable lives, serving God to the best of their ability, often inspiring great faith in others.

New Orleans Saints running back George Rogers overcame drug problems to once again become a feared ball carrier with Washington, helping the Redskins win a Super Bowl in the process. Saints wide receiver Danny Abramowicz leaves the game and devotes considerable energy to philanthropic causes and Church endeavors. Just as Saint Monica became the mother of another saint, her son Augustine, Archie Manning is the proud father of two NFL quarterbacks, Peyton of the Indianapolis Colts and Eli of the New York Giants.

Of course, it's true that other football greats have been guilty of decidedly unsaintly behavior. Curly Lambeau used college players illegally and the Green Bay Packers had to quit the American Professional Football Association. Paul Hornung and Alex Karras were suspended for gambling. Players are accused of using steroids, arrested while driving under the influence of alcohol, accused of murder, suspended for failing drug tests. Former Seattle owner Ken Behring tried to move the Seahawk franchise to Los Angeles under the cover of darkness.

However, football is larger than players; faith trumps perfidy. For the sport, fans appreciate the traditions of the game and how it brings them together as community. This group identity that team supporters form is stronger than wins and losses, injuries or disappointments. It provides for a common ground of communication, of relating, of rejoicing, or commiserating with one another. As for Christianity, it has survived reformations and denominational disagreements, even reports that God is dead.

Sometimes we forget that saints are also people. By their examples, they show us what we too are capable of accomplishing in the name of God. In the Apostles' Creed, the faithful profess a belief in "the communion of saints," the body of all souls destined for paradise. As I've mentioned, Christians believe that we are all born in the image and likeness of God. Christ died for our sins and showed us the way home. All of which is another way of saying that just as we are all sinners, we all have the capacity to be saints. We can all be a part of 'dem saints in heaven.

Hallelujah!

THE PARABLE
OF THE RAMS

RECALL JESUS' PARABLE OF THE LOST SHEEP: A shepherd rejoiced over finding the wayward animal, much as God the Father will rejoice when a repentant sinner rejoins his flock.

Here now is the parable of the won and lost Rams.

At first glance it would seem unusual that a football team might teach us anything remotely biblical. But upon closer examination we should not be surprised to learn that the team that does is a particular edition of the Rams. After all, the team in question is from *Saint* Louis.

At the close of the 1998 season, the Rams found themselves in last place in the NFC West division with a 4–12 record. One year later their fortunes were considerably better. After trading for multipurpose back Marshall Faulk in the off-season and turning the quarterbacking duties over to former grocery stockboy Kurt Warner, the Rams took the football world by storm. With Faulk's ability to elude tacklers and Warner's long bombs to fleet-footed, sure-handed receivers such as Isaac Bruce and Torry Holt, the Rams offense became known as the Greatest Show on Turf. Lo and behold, the Rams finished the season in first place in their division with a 13–3 mark. Three playoff wins later and St. Louis found itself in Super Bowl XXXIV facing the Titans of Tennessee. In an exciting game, the Rams took the lead with less than two minutes left to play, 23–16. A game-saving tackle on the last play of the contest kept the Titans one yard away from scoring the potential game-winning touchdown and extra point. Not only had the Rams won the Super Bowl, they had fulfilled in grand fashion a biblical prediction:

"...the last will be first" (Matthew 20:16).

Other football teams have done the same, most recently the New England Patriots who won the first of their three Super Bowls in four years after finishing in the cellar. In 2000 the Pats completed a disappointing season at 5–11, good (or bad) enough for last place in the AFC East. In a complete reversal, the next year the team finished 11–5 en route to their 20–17 victory over St. Louis in Super Bowl XXXVI. Going the Rams one better (or worse), New England not only finished last the year before winning it all, they had also finished last two years before winning it all.

If the Rams were worst to first, then the Pats were worst to worst to first. However, the Bears were worst to worst to worst to worst to first! Well, not quite first in that they didn't win the Super Bowl, but first in that they captured the NFC Central crown in 2001 after four straight cellar-dwelling seasons.

Cincinnati had a pair of worst to (almost) firsts. In 1980 they finished in last place in the AFC Central at 6–10, only to gain (but lose) the Super Bowl a year later. In 1987, the Bengals had another disappointing campaign, compiling a 4–11 record. However, the next season found them in the Super Bowl, unfortunately coming up short again.

Of course, Jesus just didn't say, "The last will be first." He said, "The last will be first, and the first last." Excellent examples of this come from the (play) books of Dallas and San Francisco.

In their storied history, Dallas has been very good (five Super Bowl championships) and very bad (several last place finishes). In 1960, their first year of existence, the Cowboys did not win a game, finishing 0-11-1. However, by 1978 the team had two NFL championships under their Cowboy belts. Dallas eventually came upon hard times again with a 3–13 record in 1988 and, as if to prove that was no fluke, a 1–15 mark a year later. Yet just three years after that, the 'Boys won the first of two consecutive Super Bowls, and the first two of three in a four-year span.

Similarly, San Francisco posted a pair of 2–14 seasons back to back. Two years later, in 1981, they went 13–3 along with capturing the first of their five Super Bowl trophies. In 1984, the 'Niners were a sterling 15–1, completing their league domination with their second Super Bowl. Recently the football has not bounced the 49ers' way. In the 2004–2005 seasons they finished 6–26, last in the NFC West both years.

In other words, the first will be last and the last will be first.

As you might imagine, Jesus had more in mind than the fortunes of football teams when preaching to the masses. His was a message not of wins and losses, but of equality.

In the parable of the workers in the vineyard (see Matthew 20:1–16), a well-known and sometimes troubling story, a vineyard owner hires workers at different times of the day yet pays them all the same wage. Laborers who worked the longest complained, as did those who worked through the heat of the day, that they should have received more than those few who hardly toiled. However, the owner paid the earliest workers exactly what they agreed upon and felt it his right to be generous with the rest. Jesus concludes the tale this way:

"So the last will be first, and the first will be last...."
"For many are called, but few are chosen" (Matthew 20:16; 22:14).

This was Christ's way of saying that all were welcome to God's banquet no matter when they came to the table. For thousands of years, the Jews had thought they had an exclusive relationship with the one true God. To hear that others, especially Gentiles, were also to be included among the saved was difficult to take. This was made all the more confusing by the fact that the Jews expected the Messiah to be a powerful political or military figure to lead them out from under their oppressors' rule. Instead, a lowly carpenter's son was telling them that even Samaritans could seek everlasting life.

As football has a number of worst to first, as well as first to worst, stories, so too does Scripture refer often to this notion of last being first and first last.

John the Baptist hinted that something special was about to happen when he quoted from Isaiah:

> *"Prepare the way of the Lord;*
> *   make his paths straight.*
> *Every valley shall be filled,*
> *   and every mountain and hill*
> *   shall be made low..."* (Luke 3:4–5).

Valleys filled and mountains lowered conjure up a level playing field. Christ said as much when discussing the scribes and Pharisees when he said:

> *"All who exalt themselves will be humbled, and all who humble themselves will be exalted"* (Matthew 23:12).

What's more, in the story of Jarius and the hemorrhaging woman, Jesus offers concrete examples of what these words mean.

> *Just then there came a man named Jarius, a leader of the synagogue. He fell at Jesus' feet and begged him to come to his house, for he had an only daughter, about twelve years old, who was dying.*
> *   ...Now there was a woman who had been suffering from hemorrhages for twelve years; and though she had spent all she had on physicians, no one could cure her. She came up behind him and touched the fringe of his clothes,*

and immediately her hemorrhage stopped. Then Jesus asked, "Who touched me?" When all denied it, Peter said, "Master, the crowds surround you and press in on you." But Jesus said, "Someone touched me; for I noticed that power had gone out from me." When the woman saw that she could not remain hidden, she came trembling; and falling down before him, she declared in the presence of all the people why she had touched him, and how she had been immediately healed. He said to her, "Daughter, your faith has made you well; go in peace."

While he was still speaking, someone came from the leader's house to say, "Your daughter is dead; do not trouble the teacher any longer." When Jesus heard this, he replied, "Do not fear. Only believe, and she will be saved." When he came into the house, he did not allow anyone to enter with him, except Peter, John, and James, and the child's father and mother. They were all weeping and wailing for her; but he said, "Do not weep; for she is not dead but sleeping." And they laughed at him, knowing that she was dead. But he took her by the hand and called out, "Child, get up!" Her spirit returned, and she got up at once (Luke 8:41–50, 54–55).

Jesus' actions spoke volumes. He showed that he didn't play favorites. His words, his compassion, were available to anyone and everyone. He responded, even loved, indiscriminately and absolutely. In this case, a ruler who possessed status, access, and power was no different than an unknown and unclean, and likely ostracized, woman in a patriarchal society. Yet each was granted an audience with the Lord. He listened to both, empathized with their respective troubles, came to their aid. Each was equal in his eyes.

As we've come to expect from Jesus, there was a lesson revealed in how he responded. One could make the case that the ruler had approached Christ formally and therefore had a right to his time.

Yet, the Lord diverted his attention from the man to minister to the afflicted woman. In effect, Jesus said that in our day-to-day activities, as we respond to our various duties and responsibilities, we are not to forget or ignore the poor, the powerless, the foreigner, the sick. Not only that, an argument could be made that by Jesus' example, we are to take care of the neglected and oppressed first before anything else.

So the last will be first, and the first last.

Christ's explanation that the last shall be first, and the first last, was not intended to be a reversal of the Jews' favored status, but rather the introduction of our equality in God's eyes. If first equals last and last equals first, then there is no first or last, only equals.

Likewise, the phrase "many are called, but few are chosen" might be considered exclusionary, that the call to join Jesus is made to many, yet few are actually accepted into his father's house. Reversing the emphasis, though, reveals just the opposite. The Jews, as the Chosen People, are few. Yet the entire rest of the world is also invited to Christ's banquet. So many are called (the rest of us) though few are chosen (the Jews). Far from being contradictory, the statements are complementary. Instead of feeling like there's no way we will ever attain union with Christ in heaven, we are being told that the reward is there for early and late laborers alike.

Whether a team is worst or first, first or last, there is something to be learned about faith. True fans will not lose faith in their team; they will not love their team any less for their performance, just as a parent would not love a child any less for a poor report card. That's not to say that fans or parents aren't disappointed, only that the bonds of the relationship, while tested, are not broken.

Ours is a contract with God. His covenant with us promises us everlasting life. All we are asked to do is love and serve God and one another. He may expect more from us than he does from others. He may even ask more of us at times than we feel we can give. He may expect more from those he has given much. But he is steadfast in the fact that his reward is available to us all if we hold up our end of the deal.

THE BLESSED TRINITY AND THEN SOME

ONE OF THE MOST PERPLEXING CONCEPTS of the Catholic faith tradition is that of the Blessed Trinity. As easy as it is to define—three persons in the one same God—it is as difficult to comprehend. Father, Son, and Spirit exist within and apart from one another. Though the Son became man, he always existed as Logos, the Word of God. As John opened his Gospel:

> *In the beginning was the Word, and the Word was with God, and the Word was God. He was in the beginning with God. All things came into being through him, and without him not one thing came into being* (1:1–3).

That the Son became man was made possible by the power of the Holy Spirit. When Mary asked Gabriel how she was to give birth since she did not know man, the messenger of God replied,

> *"The Holy Spirit will come upon you, and the power of the Most High will overshadow you; therefore the child to be born will be holy; he will be called Son of God"* (Luke 1:35).

Thank heaven there is football to help us grasp this mysterious concept.

Through a special relationship that certain players have with one another by virtue of the positions they play, one can perhaps get a little better understanding of the Blessed Trinity. Think of Peyton Manning, Marvin Harrison, and Edgerrin James of the Indianapolis Colts.

Manning, Harrison, and James. Quarterback, receiver, and running back. With skills that complement one another, the three opened up a high-octane offense worthy of the city that gives us the Indy 500. In the seven years (1999–2005) they played together, statisticians worked overtime. Manning threw for more than 4,000 yards six years in a row. In 2004, he set the record with most touchdown passes thrown in a single season with 49. Harrison caught more than 100 passes four consecutive seasons, and surpassed 1,100 receiving yards for seven. In 2002, he set his NFL mark with 143 catches in a season. For his part, James rushed for more than 1,200 yards in five of those seasons, and likely would have the other two had he not suffered a knee injury.

Though they helped the Colts post a combined 77–35 record, in effect winning two of every three games they played, this trio never made it to the Super Bowl. Even though Manning and Harrison claimed championship rings in Super Bowl XLI, James was not part of that team, having signed with the Arizona Cardinals for the 2006 season, bringing an end to one of the most productive trios in the history of the NFL.

While the Colt trinity never won a championship, there have been three threesomes who have helped their teams to the Promised Land. In 1975 and again in 1978 Terry Bradshaw, Lynn Swann, and Franco Harris led the Steelers in their respective categories of passing, receiving, and rushing. They also won Super Bowls at the end of those seasons. Steeler fans will no doubt point out that the black-and-gold also captured two other NFL championships during the nine seasons (1974–1982) that the three teammates played together. True, but during those years, Swann was not the team's leading receiver.

In the six seasons (1985–1990) that they played together, 49er greats Joe Montana, Jerry Rice, and Roger Craig excelled. In 1989, Montana was near perfect, throwing for more than 3,500 yards and 26 scores, while completing an astounding 70.2 percent of his passes. Of course, racking up completions is easy when you have the greatest receiver of all time at the other end of your passes, as well as one of the best ever past-catching running backs. Rice posted five years of more than 1,000 yards in receptions during this period. In 1985, Craig became the first player in NFL history to amass more than 1,000 yards rushing and receiving. Together the three San Francisco teammates helped the 49ers win back-to-back Super Bowls in 1989 and 1990.

As impressive as the offensive pyrotechnics of the three Colts or the Super Bowl winning exploits of the Steeler and 49er trios have been, perhaps no three players complemented one another better than The Triplets.

Of course, I mean Dallas Cowboys quarterback, receiver, and running back Troy Aikman, Michael Irvin, and Emmitt Smith. In their ten years together, Aikman threw for more than 3,000 yards five times, Irvin had more than 1,000 yards receiving seven times, and Smith rushed for more than 1,000 yards nine times. Each was an All-Pro several times over. And as most fans know, Emmitt Smith set the all-time NFL record for career rushing yards, with more than 18,000. To put this in perspective, that's more than ten miles. Now most people would have trouble simply toting a football that far. Try doing it will eleven guys trying to tackle you every step of the way!

What sets The Triplets apart, however, are, appropriately, three NFL trophies. In the span of four years, Dallas captured three Super Bowls: XXVII, XXVIII, and XXX. Only New England has matched this feat, but not with a single quarterback, receiver, and running back leading the way.

Even more noteworthy is how each set of triplets instructs us on the relationships among another threesome—the Father, Son, and Spirit of the Blessed Trinity.

An age-old football maxim is that a team cannot have a productive passing game without establishing an effective running game—and vice versa. Furthermore, a running back cannot rush with the ball without a handoff from the quarterback. A pass completion does not exist without a quarterback and a receiver. In short, quarterback, receiver, and running back are inextricably linked. Each position exists on its own yet, like a poorly thrown pass, is incomplete without the others.

On another level, the three positions give fans different entry points in which to embrace the game. One fan may appreciate a strong-armed quarterback; another may prefer an expert field general. A third might cheer the power of a bulldozing runner, still another finds delight in the elusive tailback. Yet a fifth may sit in awe of a wideout's speed and acrobatic maneuvers, while others praise a receiver's precise routes and sure hands.

One of our primary quests in life is to find ourselves in right relationship with God. However, God is unfathomable; we can truly never comprehend the entity that the Bible describes as "I am." So we look for ways that we can relate to the Almighty given our human limitations. We may find God in the beauty of a sunset or the joy of a child's laugh. We may relate to the "Force be with you" or pray to the three persons of the Blessed Trinity.

Far be it from me to try to explain in a few paragraphs what theologians have devoted the better part of two millennia trying to understand. Three distinct persons in the same God is a mystery to be sure. But it is also a blessing. For in each of the three persons, we have the opportunity to come to know the one God better. In God the Father, we pray to the creator of all that is. Through God the Son, we are able to forge a relationship with Jesus who walked the earth and died for our sins. Through the Spirit comes all our awareness of God and his love from us.

There are a number of references in Scripture that reveal the unique relation of these "triplets" to one another.

And Jesus came and said to them, "All authority in heaven and on earth has been given to me. Go therefore and make disciples of all nations, baptizing them in the name of the Father and of the Son and of the Holy Spirit..." (Matthew 28:18–19).

When John the Baptist baptized Jesus in the Jordan River, all three persons of the Trinity were present.

In those days Jesus came from Nazareth of Galilee and was baptized by John in the Jordan. And just as he was coming up out of the water, he saw the heavens torn apart and the Spirit descending like a dove on him. And a voice came from heaven, "You are my Son, the Beloved; with you I am well pleased" (Mark 1:9–11).

Don't worry if you have trouble grasping the concept of the Blessed Trinity. After all, Jesus' own disciples, men who had been with him day in and day out hearing him teach and preach, did not fully understand.

Philip said to him, "Lord, show us the Father, and we will be satisfied." Jesus said to him, "Have I been with you all this time, Philip, and you still do not know me? Whoever has seen me has seen the Father. How can you say, 'Show us the Father'? Do you not believe that I am in the Father, and the Father is in me? The words that I say to you I do not speak on my own; but the Father who dwells in me does his works. Believe me that I am in the Father and the Father is in me; but if you do not, then believe me because of the works themselves" (John 14:8–11).

There are times in our lives when we pray to God by way of each person of the Trinity, instances when each person offers a gateway to God. At the birth of a child, ecstatic parents thank creator God profusely for the miracle they hold in their hands. At times of temptation or frustration, we may pray to Jesus for the strength to endure the human journey, knowing that Christ faced most of the same experiences we do. When seeking how to best serve God with the talents he has given us, we seek guidance from the Spirit. In each case, we converse with a distinct person of the Trinity at the same time we forge a relationship with the one God.

To grasp the Trinity, think back to our trios. Three players tied to one another, each possessing a unique gift. Quarterback, receiver, and running back offer fans everywhere three different ways to embrace the game, just as Father, Son, and Holy Spirit offer the faithful three distinct ways to relate to the one, same God.

After all, whether it's the two-minute warning or the end of the world, it's not so much how we have come to believe, it's that we do believe.

GOATS AND LAMBS

AS BRIEFLY DISCUSSED DURING HALFTIME, football is a game of measurement and accomplishment. A field of play measures 100 yards by 53 ⅓ yards, with an additional 20 yards split between the two end zones. Hall of Famers Joe Perry and Lenny Moore posted similar numbers, though from different positions. Known as "The Jet," fullback Perry gained a combined 12,532 yards from rushing, receiving, and returns, primarily with the 49ers. Moore posted his total of 12,451 combined yards as a flanker and tailback with the Baltimore Colts. Linebackers Dick Butkus and Ray Nitschke wreaked havoc from the middle of the field for the Chicago Bears and Green Bay Packers, respectively. Butkus totaled 22 interceptions and 27 fumble recoveries as perhaps the most feared Monster of the Midway. For his part, Nitschke racked up 25 picks and 20 recoveries. Yet Ray picked up a number of championship rings with the Pack while Mr. Butkus got bupkis with "da Bears." Spending most of his career with the Buffalo Bills, Bruce Smith sacked opposing quarterbacks 200 times, while Reggie White with the Eagles and Packers got up close and personal with QBs on 198 occasions.

Americans are fascinated with comparisons, especially rankings that allow for the proclamation of Number One or the GOAT, as in the Greatest Of All Time. Business magazines routinely run articles on the top one hundred richest people in the United States. Every movie studio hopes their next summer blockbuster will unseat *Titanic* as the highest-grossing motion picture of all time ($1.8 billion worldwide).[1] Dallas, Pittsburgh, and San Francisco have all won five Super Bowls each, the most of any franchise.

What makes sports so intriguing, apart from which team will win and which team will lose, is comparing great players from different eras to arrive at just such a declaration of who is the best of the best. Fans being fans, it's only natural to want to see who is the best. Like it or not, that's why we keep score, tabulate rushing yardage, and figuring out quarterback ratings.

Sidebar: To be honest, most armchair quarterbacks do not spend much time, if any, calculating QB ratings. While not rocket science, it certainly is close to aeronautical engineering. Four categories are used to compile a passer's rating: percentage of completions per attempt, average yards gained per attempt, percentage of touchdown passes per attempt, and percentage of interceptions per attempt.[2] The highest score in any one category is 2.375; the lowest is 0.000, and the average is 1.000. To score a perfect 2.375 in any area, a quarterback must perform at an extremely high level. For instance, to earn a perfecto in completions, he must connect on 77.5 percent of his passes. To make the ratings somewhat understandable (as if that's possible), the totals are converted into a scale of 100. So it is that 'Niner quarterback Steve Young holds the career passing rating record of 96.8, while Colts QB Peyton Manning holds the single-season mark of 121.1.

From quarterback ratings to most consecutive 1,000-yard seasons rushing to most consecutive games catching at least one pass, football keeps track of the best in any number of categories. But that shouldn't be too surprising. After all, in Jesus' time, the apostles also jockeyed for top billing.

James and John, the sons of Zebedee, came forward to him and said to him, "Teacher, we want you to do for us whatever we ask of you." And he said to them, "What is it you want me to do for you?" And they said to him, "Grant us to sit, one at your right hand and one at your left, in your glory" (Mark 10:35–37).

When the ten heard it, they were angry with the two brothers (Matthew 20:24).

Perhaps the other apostles were embarrassed at the brothers' effrontery. (For example, in his Gospel, John referred to himself as "the disciple whom Jesus loved.") But it's more likely that they themselves wanted the exalted positions next to Jesus. After all, Luke did report that, *A dispute also arose among them as to which one of them was to be regarded as the greatest* (Luke 22:24).

Which just goes to show that whether twelve apostles gather or a dozen Hall of Famers, eventually talk is going to get around to who's number one. In the football world at least, a case can be made for several of the game's giants—and if not Giants, then certainly Browns and 'Niners, Cowboys and Broncos.

For sheer statistical amazement, Miami Dolphins quarterback Dan Marino has to be considered among the all-time greats. "Dan the Man" threw for more yards than any other quarterback ever to play in the NFL. As calculated earlier, his 61,361 yards passing is the equivalent of nearly thirty-five miles! Of his 4,967 completions, a phenomenal 420 went for touchdowns. He was the only quarterback to throw for more than 5,000 yards in one season, and surpassed the 3,000-yard per season mark thirteen times. The only thing missing from Marino's resumé is a Super Bowl ring, as he and the rest of his fish teammates came up short in Super Bowl XIX against San Francisco.

Since the object of the game is to win not only games but championships, perhaps Marino will have to move over for John Elway. As reported earlier, as the leader of the Denver Broncos, Elway amassed 51,475 yards and a neat 300 touchdowns. His ability to scramble to buy time and his seemingly astonishing ability to orchestrate come-from-behind victories added to his near-mythic legend. What may give him the edge over Marino in some football minds is the fact that Elway led the blue-and-orange to back-to-back victories in Super Bowls XXXII and XXXIII, helping Denver fans everywhere feel much more than a mile high.

If Super Bowl victories become the criterion on which greatness is based, then quarterbacks Tom Brady, Terry Bradshaw, and Joe Montana should throw their helmets into the championship ring. In his six seasons, Tom Brady has brought three Super Bowl trophies to New England. Along the way he has thrown for more than 21,564 yards and 147 touchdowns. Who knows how many more victories in Roman numeral games he might engineer before his career comes to a close. For now, Bradshaw and Montana hold the mark for leading their teams to Super Bowl victories with four each. Steeler Bradshaw retired with nearly 28,000 yards passing and 244 touchdowns, 212 of which came "threw" the air. Montana collected three Super Bowl MVP awards along with regular season passing totals of 40,551 yards, 3,409 completions, and 273 scoring passes. His 92-yard directed scoring drive in the closing seconds of Super Bowl XXIII is considered one of the all-time Super Bowl highlights.

What about overall championships, not just Super Bowl titles? After all, there was a great deal of football played before the advent of the Super Bowl in 1967. As mentioned, Bart Starr led the Green Bay Packers to six championships in seven years, including the first two Super Bowls. And Cleveland Browns great Otto Graham directed the Browns to ten straight title games, winning four AAFC and three NFL championship games in the process.

Still, when judging quarterbacks, for every pass they throw there is someone there to catch it. Dan Marino had Mark Duper and Mark Clayton. John Elway had Rod Smith. For Terry Bradshaw it was John Stallworth and Lynn Swann; for Joe Montana, Freddie Solomon and Dwight Clark, Jerry Rice and John Taylor. One could argue that the GOAT award should go to a running back, for once they're handed the ball, eleven defensive players are looking to take their heads off. With this in mind we are required to look at the legal-sounding threesome of (Barry) Sanders, (Walter) Payton, and (Emmitt) Smith.

As we've seen, in the course of his incredible ten-year career Barry Sanders rushed for 15,269 yards, averaging a remarkable five yards a carry. Had he not retired in his prime, many hold that he would have easily set the NFL record for most yards gained rushing in a career. Unfortunately, in football as in faith, we are judged by deeds not intentions or, in Sanders' case, potential. So in terms of being the greatest, Sanders will forever be one of the most popular topics of conversation when considering what might have been.

Walter Payton, on the other hand, retired after thirteen seasons as the game's leading rusher, compiling 16,726 yards on the ground. Between rushing scores and receptions, he totaled 125 TDs. Not only that, he threw for eight touchdowns on halfback option plays. There are those who will argue that Sanders with his 5.0 yards per carry was a better runner than Payton, who "only" averaged 4.4 yards. But none will dispute the impact Payton had on the game and the authoritative way he ran with the ball. To football fans in general and Bear fans in particular, Payton was "Sweetness" personified.

To date, Emmitt Smith is unsurpassed as the league's leading rusher. In his fifteen years, Smith amassed 18,355 yards, averaging 4.2 yards per touch. Even more impressive is his mark of eleven seasons in a row rushing for more than a 1,000 yards. Not as flashy as Sanders nor as powerful as Payton, Smith nonetheless proved to be a durable rushing machine, demonstrating that often it's not the spectacular that will win out, but the consistent, a notion in which the faith-filled among us can take heart.

Just as inflation has caused the value of the Green Bay Packers franchise to soar from only $250 to $911,000,000, so too have the game's statistics been affected. Today, NFL teams play sixteen games during the regular season. Back in the day, teams only played fourteen. Further back in the day, they only played twelve. With this in mind, Jim Brown's career takes on new meaning. Brown played just nine years before abruptly retiring. Four of those years, the NFL only played twelve games a season; the last five years of his career saw him on the field fourteen games per campaign. As referred to earlier, Jim Brown posted hard-to-believe numbers: 12,312 career rushing yards for a 5.2-yard average. To understand this more completely, examine two of his years in particular. In 1958, Brown gained 1,527 yards over twelve games. Five years later, he totaled 1,863 yards over fourteen. That's an average of 5.9 and 6.4 yards a carry, respectively. Put another way, football fans witnessed a man playing among boys. To put these amazing feats in perspective, for a sixteen-game season Brown's 1958 total would become 2,031 yards; his 1963 season would expand to 2,124. Only four players in NFL history have rushed for more than 2,000 yards a season. And no one has ever done it twice. As a Los Angeles Ram, Eric Dickerson posted the single-season rushing record with 2,105 yards, which would have fallen short of Brown's pro-rated best. No wonder many experts consider Jim Brown the Greatest Of All Time.

There are others who judge the greatest by how much they have outperformed others at the same position. With this in mind, one can make an open-and-shut case for Jerry Rice being the indisputable GOAT. In terms of passes caught, Rice grabbed 448 more balls than second-place Cris Carter, 1,549 to 1,101. For many wideouts who played the game, 448 receptions alone would have been a wonderful career. When comparing total yards via receptions, second-place Tim Brown came nearly 8,000 yards short. Again, many receivers would take just the difference in yards and consider their careers remarkable. Art Monk of the Redskins caught at least one pass in 164 consecutive games. This is an amazing feat until, that is, compared to Rice's record 274 games in a row. The difference in games represents nearly six additional seasons of catching at least one pass in a game. Throughout his twenty-year career, Jerry Rice proved to be as gracious as he was graceful, as strong as he was swift, as dedicated as he was brilliant. Yet even though he dominated his position for decades, even though he retired with near-countless entries in the NFL record book, even though he owns four Super

Bowl rings and a number of Super Bowl receiving records, he may
not be the greatest of all time.

Especially when we define greatness as Jesus does.

In responding to the qualities of greatness, Jesus said, *"...who-
ever wishes to be great among you must be your servant"* (Matthew
20:26). No other football players serve their teammates more than
offensive linemen. They open holes for the Smiths and Sanders of the
world, and provide pass protection for the Montanas and Marinos.
They operate in "the trenches," going one-on-one with massive defensive linemen. Aching knees and gnarled, bloody fingers are their
reward. At least defensive linemen receive accolades for quarterback
sacks, the occasional interception or fumble recovery, and return for
a touchdown. Unless an offensive lineman is fortunate enough to
recover one of his own players' fumbles, fans may not ever hear his
name. If an offensive lineman is mentioned, it's usually associated
with a holding penalty. Then sixty thousand people at the game and
millions more watching on television immediately know that he is
to blame for something done wrong.

Sure, there are offensive linemen who receive a modicum of attention. Green Bay Packers guard Jerry Kramer garnered praise for
a block that allowed quarterback Bart Starr to score the winning
touchdown against Dallas in the 1967 NFC Championship game.
Often referred to as the Ice Bowl, it may very well have been the
coldest football game ever played, with temperatures at –13 degrees
and a wind chill of –46.[3] In 1973, the offensive line of the Buffalo
Bills was hailed as The Electric Company, for they turned on "The
Juice," that is O. J. Simpson, who that season became the first player
ever to rush for more than 2,000 yards. But for the most part,
members of the O-Line toil in anonymity, doing the dirty work, the
heavy lifting, sacrificing their bodies to allow colleagues to achieve
individual success and teams to win championships. Theirs is indeed
a career of service.

Yet despite the gaudy statistics put up by Hall of Famers, and
the level of sacrifice given by offensive linemen, one player above

all others took the notion of service to the ultimate and, if we are to believe Jesus as quoted in Matthew, has so earned the honor of being called Great.

After four standout years as a defensive back for the Arizona Cardinals, Pat Tillman was offered a three-year, $3.6 million contract. As it happened, the contract offer came just months after the 9/11 terrorist attacks. So moved by the events of that day, Tillman turned down the contract in order to join the U.S. Army to serve our country in Iraq and Afghanistan. As patriotic as that action was, it became even more heroic when Tillman was killed by friendly fire in Afghanistan. Pat Tillman had joined the army to help protect our country from terrorists. In a tragically ironic twist of fate, he was killed by members of his own forces.

Jesus taught his apostles that, *"No one has greater love than this, to lay down one's life for one's friends"* (John 15:13). We may not realize it, but we all do this in little ways. Parents give of themselves to raise their children. Clergy give of their lives to minister to their flocks. Missionaries give of themselves in the service of the less fortunate. Christ demands of us that we serve others, that we give of ourselves, of our livelihoods, of our lives to those near and far. Just as he did on the cross. We may do what we can. We may have the potential to do more. In any case, we can all learn from Pat Tillman.

It was in the service of others that Mr. Tillman died. It was in the service of his fellow NFL players, their wives, their children. It was in the service of his country—for you and me and our loved ones. That the Cardinal defensive back was a great ballplayer was secondary to his being a great human being.

None other than Jesus himself taught us the value of sacrifice. In fact, John the Baptist had an inkling of the sacrifice that Christ would make on our behalf.

The next day [John] saw Jesus coming toward him and declared, "Here is the Lamb of God who takes away the sin of the world!" (1:29).

To live a good life, it's not enough to excel in one's profession. We must also strive to excel as human beings—to respect others, to offer care and service and love. As Jesus said, *"For what will it profit them if they gain the whole world but forfeit their life?"* (Matthew 16:26).

Put another way, for us to be considered the GOAT, we must first be a lamb.

ALAN AMECHE AND THE POWER OF FORGIVENESS

AT THE RISK OF OVERSTATING MY CASE, football can be considered a microcosm for life. Every play, like every day, represents a struggle, a challenge to succeed, to do the right thing, to make the correct choice. We are assailed from all sides with obstacles. We may move forward on our spiritual path, we may be tackled for a loss. We may trip and stumble along the way. At some point we might fumble. Angels and devils battle for our conscience as offense and defense do for the ball. Temptation forces everyone to choose, even Christ.

> *Jesus, full of the Holy Spirit, returned from the Jordan and was led by the Spirit in the wilderness, where for forty days he was tempted by the devil. He ate nothing at all during those days, and when they were over, he was famished. The devil said to him, "If you are the Son of God, command this stone to become a loaf of bread." Jesus answered him, "It is written, 'One does not live by bread alone.'"*
>
> *Then the devil led him up and showed him in an instant all the kingdoms of the world. And the devil said to him, "To you I will give their glory and all this authority; for it has been given over to me, and I give it to anyone I please. If you, then, will worship me, it will all be yours." Jesus answered him, "It is written,*

'Worship the Lord your God,
   and serve only him.'"
   Then the devil took him to Jerusalem, and placed him on
the pinnacle of the temple, saying to him, "If you are the Son
of God, throw yourself down from here, for it is written:
   'He will command his angels concerning you,
      to protect you,'
and
   'On their hands they will bear you up,
      so that you will not dash your foot against a stone.'"
Jesus answered him, "It is said, 'Do not put the Lord your
God to the test.'" When the devil had finished every test, he
departed from him until an opportune time (Luke 4:1–13).

Of course, we have not been born without sin or without the tendency to sin as Jesus was. While we are created in the image and
likeness of God, we are not God. We are but human, not human and
divine. So sin we do. But in his infinite goodness, God has provided
the antidote to sin in the form of his son, Jesus Christ and, in my
case, Alan Ameche.

Earlier, when discussing quarterback great Johnny Unitas, reference was made to what many consider to be "the greatest game ever
played"—the 1958 NFL Championship overtime thriller between
the Baltimore Colts and New York Giants. Though I was only eight
years old when the contest took place, I remember it well.

Thanks to football trading cards, I was familiar with players
from both teams. Baltimore boasted such stars as Johnny Unitas,
Lenny Moore, Alan Ameche, Raymond Berry, Jim Mutscheller,
Art Donovan, Jim Parker, Gino Marchetti, and Gene "Big Daddy"
Lipscomb. New York had such Giants of the game as Charlie Con-
erly, Frank Gifford (later of *Monday Night Football* fame), Alex
Webster, Kyle Rote, Andy Robustelli, the Roseys (Brown and Grier),
Sam Huff, and Pat Summerall (later long-time announcing partner
of John Madden). Thanks to the relatively new (in our household

anyway) marvel of television, I had a front-row seat to the game.

With my football cards at my side, I sat transfixed in front of grainy black-and-white images as the Colts and Giants battled to a 17–all tie at the end of regulation play. The game was going to sudden-death overtime; the first team that scored would become champions of the NFL, and the world for that matter. Unitas expertly led the Colts downfield, the drive climaxing with a one-yard plunge by Colts fullback Alan "The Horse" Ameche.

Little did I know at the time that Ameche would play a part in my learning of the power of forgiveness. First, some biblical background.

Since the earliest of times, humanity has been prone to sin. From Adam's and Eve's fall to Cain's murder of Abel to Moses' killing of the Egyptian overseer to David's tryst with Bathsheba, the Old Testament records its fair share of human errors. With Christ's death and resurrection, humanity's collective soul was washed clean of the stain of sin. Though our propensity to err is still in place, we have gained through Jesus everlasting forgiveness.

Thus, one of the most important lessons Christ imparted to his disciples was the notion of forgiveness. In his dying, Christ conquered sin and death; in his living he showed us the way to the kingdom of heaven. To follow Jesus was, simply, to forgive, a lesson he learned from the Father.

...for your Father knows what you need before you ask him.
　"Pray then in this way:
　Our Father in heaven,
　hallowed be your name.
　Your kingdom come.
　Your will be done,
　　on earth as it is in heaven.
　Give us this day our daily bread.
　And forgive us our debts,
　　as we also have forgiven our debtors.

> *And do not bring us to the time of trial,*
> *but rescue us from the evil one.*
> *For if you forgive others their trespasses, your heavenly*
> *Father will also forgive you; but if you do not forgive*
> *others, neither will your Father forgive your trespasses"*
> (Matthew 6:8–15).

Debts. Trespasses. In a word, sins—that comprehensive, sometimes nebulous, category of our thoughts and actions that creates distance in our relationship with God and one another. Fortunately, God loves us so much, he continually forgives us of our wrongdoings. Through that mercy, we come to know his love. In the same way that God forgives us, we too are to pardon others. Christ elaborates in the following from Mark and Luke.

> *"Whenever you stand praying, forgive, if you have anything against anyone; so that your Father in heaven may also forgive you your trespasses. But if you do not forgive, neither will your Father in heaven forgive..."* (Mark 11:25–26).

> *"Do not judge, and you will not be judged; do not condemn, and you will not be condemned. Forgive, and you will be forgiven..."* (Luke 6:37).

That's not to say forgiving is easy. While perhaps grasping the notion of forgiveness, the apostles failed, if Peter is any indication, to understand the all-encompassing notion of Forgiveness. That is, to forgive time and time again until the end of time.

> *Then Peter came and said to him, "Lord, if another member of the church sins against me, how often should I forgive? As many as seven times?" Jesus said to him, "Not seven times, but, I tell you, seventy-seven times"* (Matthew 18:21–22).

In the Bible the number seven equals more than a quantity between six and eight; it conveys abundance. So by forgiving someone seven times, Peter felt he was being more than generous. Christ's reply of "seventy-seven" is the equivalent of our "infinity times infinity," a biblical version of the new math.

Why forgiveness?

Forgiveness is the tie that binds. It closes distances and heals wounds. It liberates one from anxiety and sorrow; it frees the other from anger, bitterness, and revenge. Imagine if the Israelis and Palestinians responded to one another with apologies instead of bullets, amends instead of bombs.

Forgiveness also paves the way for our relationship with God. It is the bridge between our inherent failings as humans and the perfection that is the Almighty. Only through God's love and forgiveness can we consider ourselves worthy of being one with the Father in heaven.

Football certainly knows of man's propensity to err. Jim Marshall runs the wrong way. Scott Norwood misses the field goal that would have given Buffalo a Super Bowl title. Passes are dropped; blocks and tackles are missed; interceptions are thrown; punts are shanked; balls are fumbled; penalties are committed.

Players know of the need for forgiveness. If grudges were carried from play to play, game to game, teams would quickly break into factions, divided against one another, instead of being unified in pursuit of their common goal. How simple it is for a wide receiver to say, "My fault" after a dropped pass. How much of a relief it is to hear in return, "No sweat, you'll make the grab next time." Would that we at home and the workplace could be as contrite, that we in the schoolyard and political arena could be as forgiving.

How important is forgiveness? During his ministry, Jesus became known as a wonder worker, a miracle man. So much so that people lost sight of his lessons to be learned. To impress upon his followers the magnitude of forgiving, Jesus often placed a greater emphasis on it than the miracles themselves.

> *Just then some men came, carrying a paralyzed man on a bed. They were trying to bring him in and lay him before Jesus; but finding no way to bring him in because of the crowd, they went up on the roof and let him down with his bed through the tiles into the middle of the crowd in front of Jesus. When he saw their faith, he said, "Friend, your sins are forgiven you." Then the scribes and the Pharisees began to question, "Who is this who is speaking blasphemies? Who can forgive sins but God alone?" When Jesus perceived their questionings, he answered them, "Why do you raise such questions in your hearts? Which is easier, to say, 'Your sins are forgiven you,' or to say, 'Stand up and walk'? But so that you may know that the Son of Man has authority on earth to forgive sins"—he said to the one who was paralyzed—"I say to you, stand up and take your bed and go to your home." Immediately he stood up before them, took what he had been lying on, and went to his home, glorifying God"* (Luke 5:18–25).

While there are many references in the Bible regarding the importance and power of forgiveness, all one really needs to know is the story of Jesus and Peter. Recall that, despite Christ's foretelling, Peter denied his Lord three times, an episode that exemplifies our own tendency to fail repeatedly despite our best intentions. Though a low point in Peter's life, the event provided Jesus an opportunity to demonstrate God's forgiveness of each of our debts, of every trespass, of all of our sins.

> *When they had finished breakfast, Jesus said to Simon Peter, "Simon son of John, do you love me more than these?" He*

said to him, "Yes, Lord; you know that I love you." Jesus
said to him, "Feed my lambs." A second time he said to
him, "Simon son of John, do you love me?" He said to him,
"Yes, Lord; you know that I love you." Jesus said to him,
"Tend my sheep." He said to him the third time, "Simon son
of John, do you love me?" Peter felt hurt because he said to
him the third time, "Do you love me?" And he said to him,
"Lord, you know everything; you know that I love you."
Jesus said to him, "Feed my sheep" (John 21:15-17).

Three times did Peter deny Jesus; three times did Christ welcome him home. So too will he welcome us home if only we but knock at his door and say, "My fault."

One might expect forgiveness on the Seas of Galilee. After all, Jesus is divine. He is above pettiness and holding a grudge. His mercy has no end. But what about forgiveness on the fields of play? At the offices of work? In the rooms of home? Many times we are so wounded by another that we are left with physical or emotional scars, anger, or the need for vengeance. Similarly, there are those occasions when we will inherently know we have done wrong, when we are so filled with remorse and shame that we have nowhere to turn except our forgiving Father.

Which brings me back to Alan Ameche.

Sometime after witnessing "the greatest game ever played," I found myself in my cousin's room trading football cards. I don't recall what transactions transpired that day. However, I do know I walked away with a brand-new Alan Ameche football card, a prized "Alan Who Rushed for the Winning Touchdown in Overtime to Win the 1958 NFL Championship for the Baltimore Colts Ameche" football card. The problem was I didn't trade for it. When my cousin wasn't looking, I swiped it.

Almost immediately I knew I had done something terrible. Not far removed from my first confession, the commandment, *thou shalt not steal*, blazed in my mind like bright neon in the dark. On the ride home I questioned my mom, without mentioning any names, as to the fate of a soul that had perished in the state of mortal sin. Her answer did little to relieve my fears. I silently and fervently prayed that my dad would not get into an accident as we drove home. This being a Saturday, I nervously checked my watch, calculating my chances to get to confession on time. Once home, I immediately mailed the offending card with a note to my cousin. In the letter I told him that I had accidentally taken Alan home with me. In short, I lied. Another sin. I hopped on my bike and raced to the confessional, where I poured out my wrongdoings to the priest who gave me penance and, best of all, absolved me of my sins. My feeling of relief was palpable. Guilt, shame, grief, anxiety, and fear all went by the wayside. In their place was tranquillity. All was right with the world. I had avoided a damning situation. Barely.

Now many might ascribe my feelings to the overly dramatic imagination of an eight-year-old, parochial school–trained, Catholic boy. Fair enough. However, that confession will live with me always.

Today, the sacrament of penance is called the sacrament of reconciliation, a far better name as the sacrament is much more than serving a penalty for doing wrong. My misadventure with Alan Ameche taught me that this sacramental ritual reconciles us with others, but also reconciles ourselves with God. we acknowledge our sinfulness and accept our Father's forgiveness. A lightness of being inevitably occurs from knowing that, though we did sin and though we may sin again, for this moment we are in right relationship with God. We glimpse the power of Christ's sacrifice for us on the cross. We feel a gratitude that is overwhelming and a love that is never ending.

For that, I have faith—and football—to thank.

RESURRECTIONS: A HOLLYWOOD ENDING

TO TEACH US FORGIVENESS was but one of many reasons that Jesus walked among humanity. He also taught us the value of good works. *"Very truly, I tell you, the one who believes in me will also do the works that I do and, in fact, will do greater works than these..."* (John 14:12).

Not only can we learn this lesson from the Bible, we see it played out every season on the gridiron. Individually, if a player does good works by blocking, tackling, throwing, running, or catching, he is rewarded in salary and awards. Shaun Alexander's $62 million contract and Brett Favre's back-to-back-to-back MVPs easily come to mind. Should enough players do good works together, the team is rewarded with postseason success and fan support, the most recent example being the Indianapolis Colts' victory in Super Bowl XLI. On a secular level, if enough citizens do good works, the community as a whole is rewarded with better schools, newer facilities for the arts, and improved services for the disadvantaged, maybe even a new state-of-the-art football stadium.

Yes, it sounds simple. Yet the combined notions of football, forgiveness, and good works help explain one of the most mysterious and glorious events in all of Christianity.

The Resurrection.

Forgiveness and good works were just pre-game drills for the Lord's true purpose here on earth. Namely, to suffer, die, be buried, and rise again. In fact, Isaiah told the Jews what Christ was going to do long before he became human.

> "Now I will rise," says the LORD,
>   "now I will lift myself up;
>   now I will be exalted..." (33:10).

Jesus himself foretold of his passion. Matthew, Mark, and Luke each noted this fact in the gospels to their respective audiences, it was that important.

> He took the twelve aside again and began to tell them what was to happen to him, saying, "See, we are going up to Jerusalem, and the Son of Man will be handed over to the chief priests and the scribes, and they will condemn him to death; they will hand him over to the Gentiles; they will mock him, and spit upon him, and flog him, and kill him; and after three days he will rise again" (Mark 10:32–34).

And so he was killed. And so he did rise.

But what was it to be crucified? In that day and age, crucifixion was a standard form of execution performed by the Romans against enemies of the empire. Those sentenced were bound or nailed to a cross, hoisted up outside the city walls in the midday sun of the Middle East, and left to die of dehydration or asphyxiation. Sometimes legs or ribs were broken to hasten the process; a sword to the side was not uncommon. Death was slow. Death was painful.

In his book, *Death on a Friday Afternoon*, Richard John Neuhaus meditates on the last words of Jesus from the cross.[1] From these seven thoughts (there's that number of plenty again), we learn every-

RESURRECTIONS: A HOLLYWOOD ENDING

thing we need to know about Jesus' mission on earth and ours.

> *"Father, forgive them; for they do not know what they are doing"* (Luke 23:34).

Who are they? Those who condemned Jesus, those who mocked him, who crucified him, who failed to believe him. Who are they? Look in the mirror. Those of us who can't help but fail him through our anger, our selfishness, our envy, our lust, our humanness. Yet, even on the cross, Jesus forgave them then and forgives us now. And asks us to do the same.

> *"Truly I tell you, today you will be with me in Paradise"* (Luke 23:43).

By his death and resurrection, Christ is leading us all home to God the Father, from the repentant thief at his side on the cross to the last one of us left standing on the planet.

> *"Woman, here is your son."..."Here is your mother"* (John 19:26–27).

Jesus was not just providing security for his mother, giving her a son in John, or even John a mother in Mary. No, it was more than that. Christ's mother is now our mother. We are her children. We are each other's sons and mothers, fathers and daughters, brothers and sisters.

> *"My God, my God, why have you forsaken me?"* (Mark 15:34).

Even in Christ's moment of desolation, in an apparent cry of abandonment, Jesus addressed God as my God. Said twice for emphasis. Though seemingly forsaken, said twice for affection.

"I am thirsty" (John 19:28).

As we all thirst, so did Jesus for the comfort of his Father, for only God can truly quench our spiritual longing.

"It is finished" (John 19:30).

Jesus said that it is finished, but not that it is over. Rather, his mission is complete. Fulfilled. Brought to perfection. With death, the stage is set to rise to the Father.

"Father, into your hands I commend my spirit" (Luke 23:46).

When Jesus sought release in the Garden from his ordeal, he prayed to his Father, *"Not my will, but yours be done."* Having consented to God's will, Jesus is now ready to be welcomed home by the Father. As we learn to do God's will in our own lives, we also prepare ourselves to be welcomed home by the Father.

Though painful and agonizing, dying was the easy part. Only when Christ rose from the dead did his disciples sense the wonder of it all, realize the miracle and mystery they had been a part of, believe without a doubt that the Son of God had walked in their midst.

So what does it all mean for us? By listening to Christ's words from the cross we learn everything we need to know to be saved: forgive others, take care of one another, thirst for spiritual union, trust in God. By being blessed by the Lord's resurrection, we are given the one thing we need to see us through our darkest days.

Hope.

Hope that despite all our fears and failures, our sins and trespasses, our human imperfections, we are forgiven. Hope that despite dreams unrealized, loves unrequited, plans disappointed, children lost, marriages torn, despite our bodies growing old and failing us, we too, through God's mercy and grace, can overcome sin, can overpower death.

Hope that there is, indeed, hope for us.

What's more, as the Bible provides us hope, remarkably so too does football. Hope abounds every summer camp when players, coaches, and fans alike look forward to a new season, with all mistakes and failed opportunities of the past erased, with renewed opportunity to reach the promised land of the Super Bowl. Hope abounds every game when Peyton Manning throws the bomb to Marvin Harrison or Adam Vinatieri lines up a field goal. Hope abounds every down when Ray Lewis lines up over the center to stuff the run. Or when Dante Hall fields a punt and sprints to daylight. Hope abounds in the off-season when the Cowboys sign Terrell Owens, the Saints ink Drew Brees, or the Titans draft Vince Young.

Resurrection gives us a chance at new life. Every day we die to God. It may be by ignoring a homeless person on the street, a cross word to a loved one, an eruption of road rage, a fist thrown in anger, a marriage betrayed. Every day, we also have a chance to be born anew, to rise again, to live as Jesus taught us, to grow closer to God, to be forgiven, to do good works.

Few other experiences in life offer us resurrection on a weekly basis as does football. Brett Favre moves from being a backup in Atlanta to a Super Bowl champion in Green Bay. Steve Young survives life in the short-lived USFL and a sack-filled tenure with Tampa Bay to lead the 49ers to their fifth Super Bowl title. Ernest Byner overcomes the heartbreak of his fumble at the goal line as a Cleveland Brown to be part of the world champion Redskins. After missing thirty-one games and nearly two years with an arm injury, Joe Montana comes back to play two more seasons.

Football is not one game or a season, just as our life is not just what happens today or this year. Neither is one stop along the way; both are an entire journey. All of us will be faced with trials of one sort or another. Sometimes we overcome our hurdles, sometimes we stumble and fall. All that God asks of us is that we do the best we can each and every time. Either way, it is enough. With success comes rejoicing. With setback comes learning, and the experience to prevail the next time.

By now it should come as no surprise that two of the most memorable stories of death and rebirth come from the gridiron.

As a Heisman Trophy winner from Stanford, quarterback Jim Plunkett was the first player selected overall in the 1970 draft. Having led Stanford to its first Rose Bowl victory since World War II, he was expected to perform a similar turnaround for the New England Patriots. His career started well enough with the Rookie of the Year award his first season. But in his next four campaigns with the Patriots, Plunkett threw more interceptions than touchdowns each season. New England gave up on the QB and shipped him to San Francisco. Since Plunkett had collegiate success in the Bay Area, the 49ers were hoping that he would respond to being home. No such luck. His two years with the 'Niners were again marked by more picks than TDs. After the 1977 season he was released, becoming one of the biggest busts in football history.

Across the Bay, the Oakland Raiders were in need of a backup quarterback and took a chance on Plunkett. In a span of two years, he only appeared in four games, completing just seven of fifteen passes. However, in 1980, after Raiders QB Dan Pastorini broke his leg, Plunkett received a chance at redemption.

In one of the most dramatic career turnarounds in NFL history, Plunkett led Oakland to nine wins in eleven games, helping the Raiders secure the wild card spot in the playoffs. Three playoff victories later, Plunkett led the silver-and-black to a 27–10 victory over the Philadelphia Eagles in Super Bowl XV. With three touchdown passes in the contest, he was named the game's Most Valuable Player. As if that wasn't enough, Plunkett again led the pride and poise boys to a world championship with a 38–9 drubbing of the Washington Redskins in Super Bowl XVIII.

It's one thing to resurrect a football career. Doing so with one's life is an entirely different matter. Yet it can be done with the help of God.

Thomas Henderson was such a star at outside linebacker for the Dallas Cowboys that he earned All-Pro honors as well as the nickname Hollywood. Unfortunately, he lived up to the fast lifestyle that name implied. His frequent episodes with drugs, alcohol, and the opposite sex took its toll on his game. Showing total disregard for his teammates and the game of football, he snorted cocaine during Super Bowl XIII. Two years later he was out of the league.

Far from being a wake-up call, his release allowed him more time to give in to his demons. In 1983, he was arrested for smoking crack cocaine in the company of two teenaged girls. Henderson was accused of threatening them with a gun and sexually assaulting them. He countered that he provided the crack for consensual sex. After pleading no contest, Henderson served eight months in court-ordered drug rehab, as well as two years in prison. This time, Henderson did wake up. He abandoned his Hollywood persona and has been clean ever since.[2]

As encouraging as this story is, there is even a more remarkable chapter. In 2000, Henderson won the $28 million Texas Lottery. Realizing what a gift he had been given, he gave in return. Henderson started the East Side Youth Services & Street Outreach charity and made donations to the East Austin community where he was raised. Currently, Thomas Henderson gives motivational speeches and conducts anti-drug seminars.[3]

Jim Plunkett overcame the "death" of a career to lead the Raiders to two Super Bowls. Thomas Henderson overcame the ruination of his playing days, addictions, and a prison sentence to give back to his community. In effect, he rose again from a self-destructive existence. Jesus rose after three days, overcoming not just interceptions or drug abuse, but the final enemy. By conquering death, the Lord gave the prospect of everlasting life to us all.

Hope.

Faith and football provide a never-ending supply of this most valuable virtue. In a world plagued by threats of war, corporate greed, death, and disease, the Bible shows us how we should conduct our lives and where comfort may be found. Every fall, football affords us all a clean slate, a new season, and renewed confidence with which to set forth for the Promised Land. If we falter, should we fail, we are given another chance next down, next quarter, next game, next season. Should we sin against the Father, he too grants us as many "snaps" as we might need to bring us to the end zone of the End Times, which is his heavenly kingdom. When we sin, we die to God; when we're forgiven, when we do good works, we are given new life.

Forever and ever.

As Jesus said, *"I am the resurrection and the life. Those who believe in me, even though they die, will live, and everyone who lives and believes in me will never die"* (John 11:25–26).

This is why we can join God and say, "It's good!"

NOTES

PRE-GAME SHOW

1. www.benmaller.com/archives/2006/may/03-bama_coach_forceed_to
   _change_churches.html.
2. Ibid.
3. *Sports Illustrated*, May 15, 2006.

CREATION: THE BIG KICKOFF

1. *Truly Xtra Large* by Chris Ryan, National football League, February 9,
   2006, www.atlantafalcons.com/team/archive.jsp?id=10807.
2. Ibid.
3. www.adherents.com/rel_USA.html#families.
4. Center for Applied Research in the Apostolate. Washington, DC: George-
   town University, 2007.
5. www.adherents.com/rel_USA.html#religions.
6. www.nfl.com/history/chronology/1869–1910.
7. Ibid.
8. Ibid.
9. Ibid. and http://en.wikipedia.org/wiki/Walter_Camp and www.walter-
   camp.org.
10. www.nfl.com/history/chronology/1869–1910.
11. Ibid.
12. Ibid.
13. Ibid.
14. www.nfl.com/history/chronology/1911–1920.
15. Ibid.
16. http://clubs.hemmings.com/clubsites/hupmobilefaq.htm.
17. www.nfl.com/history/chronology/1921–1930.

18. Ibid.
19. www.nfl.com/history.1931–1940.
20. *Hearts on Fire: Praying with Jesuits*, edited by Michael Harter, SJ, The Institute of Jesuit Sources, St. Louis, Missouri, 1993, page 34.

THE GOOD BOOK AND THE PLAYBOOK I

1. www.nfl.com/history/chronology/1911–1920.
2. www.nfl.com/history/chronology/1921–1930.
3. www.forbes.com/lists/2006/30/06nfl_Green-Bay-Packers_302814.html.
4. www.nfl.com/history/chronology/1921–1930.
5. www.lambeaufield.com/stadium_info/history/.
6. Ibid.
7. http://espn.go/pge2/s/superbowlmoments10.html.
8. www.profootballhof.com/hof/member.jsp?player_id=29 and http://en.wikipedia.org/wiki/George_Blanda.
9. www.profootballhof.com/hof/member.jsp?player_id=21.
10. www.profootballhof.com/hof/member.jsp?player_id=77.
11. www.profootballhof.com/hof/member.jsp?player_id=126.
12. www.profootballhof.com/hof/member.jsp?player_id=221.
13. www.profootballhof.com/hof/member.jsp?player_id=219.

PROVERBS, PROPHETS, AND PRO FOOTBALL

1. www.profootballhof.com/hof/member.jsp?player_id=104.
2. www.profootballhof.com/hof/member.jsp?player_id=25.

THE GOOD BOOK AND THE PLAYBOOK II

1. http://en.wikipedia.org/wiki/The_Catch_(American_football).
2. www.nfl.com/history/chronology/1921–1930.
3. www.nfl.com/history/chronology/1911–1920.

THE DRAFT: PLAYERS AND APOSTLES

1. www.nfl.com/history/chronology/1911–1920.
2. www.nfl.com/history/chronology/1931–1940.
3. http://en.wikipedia.org/wiki/Ryan_Leaf.

PLAYERS AND PARABLES

1. www.profootballhof.com/history/decades/1980s/eric_dickerson.jsp.
2. www.profootballhof.com/history/decades/1980s/eric_dickerson.jsp.

NOTES

TALENTS AND TOUCHDOWNS

1. www.profootballhof.com/hof/member.jsp?player_id=188.

FUM-BLE!

1. www.nfl.com/history/chronology/1869–1910.
2. http://en.wikipedia.org/wiki/Holy_Roller_(American_football).
3. http://en.wikipedia.org/wiki/The_Miracle_at_the_Meadowlands.
4. http://en.wikipedia.org/wiki/The_Fumble.
5. http://en.wikipedia.org/wiki/Brian_Sipe.
6. http://en.wikipedia.org/wiki/Jackie_Smith.
7. http://en.wikipedia.org/wiki/National_Football_League_lore#1960s.

HALFTIME

1. Killgallon, Rev. James, and Rev. Gerard Weber, et al., *Life in Christ: A Catholic Catechism for Adults*, ACTA Publications, 1995, pages 244, 245, 246.
2. Ibid., pages 246–247.
3. Ibid., page 247.
4. Pennock, Michael Francis, *The Seeker's Catechism: The Basics of Catholicism*, Ave Maria Press, Notre Dame, Indiana, 1994, page 45.

THE IMMACULATES

1. http://en.wikipedia.org/wiki/Immaculate_Reception.
2. Ibid.
3. Ibid.
4. Ibid.

HAIL MARY: FROM PRAYER BOOK TO PLAYBOOK

1. http://en.wikipedia.org/wiki/Hail_Mary.
2. http://en.wikipedia.org/wiki/Hail_Mary_pass.
3. Ibid.

GENTILES AND THE AMERICAN FOOTBALL LEAGUES

1. www.nfl.com/history/chronology/1921–1930.
2. www.nfl.com/history/chronology/1931–1940.
3. Ibid.
4. www.nfl.com/history/chronology/1941–1950.
5. Ibid.

NOTES

A TALE OF TWO PAULS

1. http://en.wikipedia.org/wiki/Paul_Brown.
2. Ibid.
3. Ibid.
4. Ibid.

OH, 'DEM SAINTS

1. http://en.wikipedia.org/wiki/Archie_Manning.
2. www.prayerguide.org.uk/stfrancis.htm.
3. www.scborromeo.org/prayers/jude2.htm.
4. www.scborromeo.org/saints/patrick.htm.
5. www.profootballhof.com/hof/member.jsp?player_id=186 and www.sf49ers .com/history/hall_of_famers.php?section=HI%20Hall%20Of%20Famers.
6. www.scborromeo.org/saints/rose.htm.
7. www.newadvent.org/cathen/14663b.htm.

GOATS AND LAMBS

1. www.imdb.com/boxoffice/alltimegross?region=world-wide.
2. http://www.nfl.com/news/981202qbrate.html.
3. http://members.cox.net/~kbrews/nflwx/grb19671231.html.

RESURRECTIONS: A HOLLYWOOD ENDING

1. Neuhaus, Richard. *Death on a Friday Afternoon: Meditations on the Last Words of Jesus from the Cross*, Basic Books, 2000.
2. http://en.wikipedia.org/wiki/Thomas_%22Hollywood%22_Henderson.
3. Ibid.

SOURCES AND PERMISSIONS

Every effort has been made to locate and secure permission for the inclusion of all copyrighted material in this book. If any such acknowledgments have been inadvertently omitted, the publisher would appreciate receiving full information so that proper credit may be given in future editions.

Scripture references are taken from the *New Revised Standard Version Bible: Catholic Edition*, copyright 1993 by the Liturgical Press, Collegeville, Minnesota. Used by permission. All rights reserved.

All football statistics come from either *www.nfl.com* or *www.pro -football-reference.com*. All efforts have been made to reflect the statistics accurately. Please accept my apologies for any errors that may have inadvertently occurred.

CPSIA information can be obtained
at www.ICGtesting.com
Printed in the USA
LVOW04s1559250416

485219LV00020B/778/P